DELAYING THE SUNSET
A STUDY OF THE ARAB WOMAN'S MIND

By Gladys Matar

Printed By Matar Books

Text copyright © 2015 by Gladys Matar
All characters, names and related indicia are trademarks of and ©
by Gladys Matar.
Delaying the Sunset Publishing Rights © Gladys Matar
All rights reserved.
Publishers since 2013
Edited by Selena Templeton
No part of this publication may be reproduced, or stored in a retrieval
system, or transmitted in any form or by any means, electronic,
mechanical, photocopying, recording, or otherwise, without written
permission of the publisher. For information regarding permission,
write to Gladys Matar, Attention: Permissions Department,
Gladyola_66@yahoo.com

Library of Congress Cataloging-in-Publication Data Available

Library of Congress Control Number: 2015919807

ISBN 978-1-939898-04-3
Printed in the U.S.A.
First American edition, November 2015

CONTENTS

DELAYING THE SUNSET

A STUDY OF THE ARAB WOMAN'S MIND

INTRODUCTION

One day I was watching a cartoon and one of the characters, a princess, wanted to "delay the sunset" with her magic crystal so that her lover could make it on time for their marriage. The moment I heard that expression, I thought about the exhausting and never-ending efforts that women go through just to "delay their sunset." And thus, the idea for this book came about.

This book is about the Arabic female mind, but it's not my intention to set woman against man, proceeding my way into unknown doom with a blindfold covering my eyes. I am not one to fanatically defend woman no matter what. In fact, I think that the most harm done to womankind has come from those who defend her without being able to see her as a partner who should, to some extent, share the responsibility for this discrimination from which she suffers. As far as I am concerned, I am in total harmony with man, who is part of my human, spiritual, cultural, and moral makeup. So I understand that we are facing exactly the same challenges, but with different approaches that are based on disparate mind structures and ways in which we view life.

The Hijab[1] phenomenon has long been considered the most controversial and sophisticated taboo when it comes to the restrictions imposed upon the Arabic female. It became, over time, another challenge that she tried desperately to deal with, either by accepting and going along with the Islamic interpretations of its concept in order to avoid a hellish injustice, or by denying it and fleeing to the other side of the river, so to speak.

However, the Hijab and all its rituals was not born from the Islamic womb, but rather is a "culture" that has been written about in detail in earlier documented texts throughout history. Author Mohja Kahf writes in her book *From Royal Body the Robe Was Removed: The Blessings of the Veil and the Trauma of Forced Unveiling in the Middle East* that "Veiling, however, did not originate with the advent of Islam. Statuettes depicting veiled priestesses precede all three Abrahamic religions (Christianity, Judaism, and Islam), dating back as far as 2500 BCE."[2]

The Hijab is not meant to be about isolation, nor to establish the difference between a free woman and a slave or prostitute, nor is it to demonstrate class discrimination. There is a far deeper reason for it: it is her mind's desire to be "invisible, not visible," as the Christian apologist Tertullian said. Thus, several questions must be asked. Is woman really willing to wear the Hijab contrary to her feelings about it? Is she trying to distance herself from the world and simply observe it through the safety of a tiny hole in her veil? Does she insist on seeing the world without being seen? Is the Hijab originally a female idea? An innate feature of her mind? And if so, why does her mind wish to go through life without being visible, exposed, and fully expressed? What makes it afraid? What are its concerns? And how did it change so entirely from the time when the matriarchal female mind dominated the whole human scene, as told in the Babylonian creation myth, "Inoma Alish"?

Well, it is no longer possible, for me at least, to see the issue of veiling as a mere sacred breach, but rather as something more problematic. I see the Hijab as the incapacity of woman's mind to deal with the fact that this promise for a better life fits only with the nature of the mind who initiated this legislation in the first place: man. Thus, we are moving away somewhat from all jurisprudent and textual interpretations about the Hijab and moving closer to the idea of dealing with the law, not as it is defined in Arabic culture as an approach (per *The Lisān al-Arab*),[3] but as a tool to legislate woman's rights in proportion to her mind that does not completely understand the world around it. If one's mind is not able to know its own essence, then implementing a law that corresponds with the nature of that very mind to keep it alive is useless. The Arabic female mind is literally not part of the Arabic mind taken in the overall sense of the word. They do not share common data passed on from their culture, nor are they on the same ideological page. The Arabic female mind is the "result" of this Arabic mind.

The Arabic female mind, as it is understood and seen with its present traits, is not just a phenomenon that evolved naturally, fed by data collected from history, geography, and popular memory, but it is also a reaction to the cultural heritage generated by the male Arabic mind. It is just like the relationship between the suppressor and the suppressed. The former decides how things should be and the latter embodies the inevitable consequence of this decision. Both suppressor and suppressed have many common traits, from provocation, manipulation, and indeterminism to a lack of initiative. And furthermore, the suppressed exhibits such attributes as self-violence which manifests as veiling or self-isolation.

Even in the absence of physical veiling and all its rituals, the structure of the female's mind does not change much, since the Hijab is still existent within the walls of her head, urging her to be invisible, but under the guise of expressing herself in a liberal and authentic way.

It is a mind that moves per the duality of "Halal"[4] and "Haram,"[5] swinging between these extremes, up and down, back and forth, left and right, again and again, without the ability to look beyond this context. Thus, it is a mind that doesn't have a full capacity to "know" without losing its way. "Knowing" is one of the most important tools of survival, and its components, as Aristotle believes, are sense, conjecture, and inference. In Plato's Theory of Forms, he states this even more clearly by saying that "knowing" constitutes sanity.

Nevertheless, it is, primarily, a suppressed mind and not a relaxed one. Therefore, it would prefer to be beholder and not visible, unidentified and not unique, passive and not active, exhausting itself in the smallest details yet not instigator of events within the orbit of their broader movements. Oppression does not stop at this point, but goes beyond mere despondency to something more painful, especially when it tends to establish a law in order to preserve its "rights," or when it intends to express itself with lack of eloquence, certainty or confidence.

In 1923, when Huda Shaarawi[6] waved her Hijab at some women gathered at the Alexandria port to welcome her back home from her trip to Europe, she shocked them by throwing her Hijab into the sea. This was not only because of her intention to urge these women to revolt against the "sacred text" by changing their outfits, but also because she wanted to put woman's mind back on its natural track, just as God created it. She wanted to purge these women's visions of all taboos and impurities so that they would know how to draft a law that would fit precisely with the spirit of their real femininity and not according to the expectations of the "official sacred speech," which had been going on for centuries.

The controversy about woman's mind is found today in this critical debate: which decree must woman reference, the sacred text or natural law? And by natural law, I mean that which derives from freedom taken at its deepest meaning, the freedom of expression and self-determination. Sir William Blackstone, an English jurist and judge, said it best: "Man...must necessarily be subject to the laws of his Creator. This will of his Maker is called the law of nature....This law of nature...is of course superior to any other.... No human laws are of any validity, if contrary to this: and such of them as are valid derive all their force...from this original."[7] Which law is the most powerful and apt to win the race in her mind?

If a hectic war were happening now so as to blow away the unjust personal and criminal laws that are based on text and jurisprudence and their extensions, does that mean that we should replace them with more prejudiced and inconsistent laws? Or with laws that are based on woman's nature as a female and originate from a mind that now knows what it wants and what its core essence is?

I offer an attempt to understand the nature of this Arabic female mind, although I am certain that there are twenty-two Arabic minds, every one of them made up of its own particular network of passages paved by local culture, verbal and written laws, the vice law, and other laws whose origins remain vague and possess ever-growing strength and persistence generation after generation.

The Arab mind has to be nourished with a secular education in order to rise from the dead, as does woman's mind. Civic culture[8] requires that the sacred text be excluded from politics and legislation. It also requires that we establish society according to the International Bill of Human Rights, not according to this bitter obsession that makes the Arabic mind wander among passed-down traditions, insisting that they are the zeitgeist of life. This effort is a wasted one, because it leads the legal system down unwanted paths, loads it beyond its ability to function, and brings about a society that is not able to progress in a way that is consistent with human rights.

Thus, I believe that the widely disseminated change that woman is being asked to adapt to today per the new modern ethical legislation consists of complete equality with man. She is being requested to program her mind to fit with the laws and theories of this policy and reshape her identity accordingly—the very thing that is disastrous to the rehabilitation of her mind. Woman's mind is different, substantively and spiritually, from man's mind, and rehabilitation can only be done by maintaining its freedom of expressing itself fully from now on. By doing so, this mind may recover from its fears and start to recognize itself and show its original and authentic features without being an effect of anything else whatsoever.

The only way to draft a new law that has completely

emerged from the uniqueness of woman in general and the Arabic woman in particular is to allow the idea of *complementation* with man, not the equality with him, to be publicized.

I mentioned in my book, *Behind the Veil of Femininity*, published in 2006, that the Arab man is miserable for he has not met a woman with a healthy, real, and free femininity, that self-expressive internal energy that moves from the inside out and not vice versa. In other words, the Arab man does not see the woman's mind exactly as created by nature, but rather an unauthentic and veiled version of it.

Achieving real knowledge and truth is a human activity that is given naturally to both man and woman without any discrimination. Many important issues such as justice, freedom, and democracy have been developed recently in Arabic culture, but when discussion about these issues began, the female mind was unable to stamp its fingerprint on it and participate fully. These matters were left to the Arabic male's mind to examine and to extract that which was most suitable for *him*, while the female mind, suffering from this historical unfairness, insisted upon one thing: equality. Practically speaking, this means that she be accepted in a kingdom wherein all laws are made for man only. The idea of equality has occupied woman's mind for a long time, but unfortunately that is not the best way to return to nature.

What is interesting, however, is that the mind of the Western woman, who has known equality for many decades, is living its own major crisis even after the sexual revolution that Western society went through. In fact, equality did not really help the Western female mind to express its own distinctiveness. Why did the sexual revolution not produce true equality? Why is this equality not reflected in the enormous freedom that Western women enjoy? The freedom of swimming in a masculine culture supported by united labor laws and unisex outfits? Where is the solution that will allow the Arabic female mind to begin to consciously recognize itself, its structure, and what it wants?

Though I will attempt to answer these questions in this book, the solution, which promises not to be simple or straight forward, may lay entirely somewhere else!

The Theory of the "Fairer Sex"

My hatred for math in high school would not let me ignore the fact that human knowledge evolved from mathematics to hypotheses via philosophy. By mathematics, I mean the numbers or statistics necessary to draft a hypothesis in the first place, such as chemistry, which became a science only when scientists could measure the substances with which they work. When I used to debate with my father about something, he requested only that I think about my viewpoint as well as its opposite with all the ensuing consequences. He would leave me to think it over carefully before I returned to him with my decision. Those debates and the desire to assert my position trained me to understand the structure of a hypothesis and to see that it starts as an idea or a mental deduction that is developed into more precise speculation through additional effort.

As I grew older, and through further research and exploration, I learned that a hypothesis addresses a theory that turns into fact so long as there are natural laws that support its "rightness," and as long as the motives of its existence still occur in full practice. At that point, the hypothesis turns into reality.

According to the Concise Dictionary of Philosophy, "For a human being to know about a subject, he has to start with noticing its external qualifications, observing its unique qualities and then he may go on delving deeper into its essence so as to elucidate the laws whereby it is governed. In this way, there would be a possibility for him to be able to explain these qualities and collect the specific data related to them in a more integrated context. This tangible and multifaceted knowledge about the subject is exactly what the theory is meant to be in its common-sense structure. But no matter if a theory is accurate and objective, it doesn't give a complete and final insight on the subject. The developed cognitive process leads to more new facts and topics, and it happens that many of these facts do not fall under the heading of the old theory, thus, they require to be changed, or to be put in a new theory setting."[9]

For example:

A truth: The illiteracy percentage among women in the Arab world is 60%.[10]

A theory: This high rate of illiteracy is the result of a prevalent belief throughout history regarding the innate nature of women.

A hypothesis, or a proposed explanation: Illiteracy among women results from lack of financial resources, availability in the workforce, or other anti-female discriminative reasons.

❦

The theory of "the fairer sex" assumes that there is an initial clear boundary of discrimination separating femininity from masculinity. The discrimination here as I see it in its simple form refers to a mere organic physiological difference. Woman tends to be weaker physically and more nurturing, while man is generally more physically powerful and emotionally inhibited. However, this gender dissimilarity is not the most important one, as the French psychoanalyst Jacques Lacan[11] states. There is another fundamental biological difference that manifests itself in both man and woman, such as sexual secretions and the genetic difference in chromosomes. But these are not really visible, for woman can "play" the role of man, and vice versa. So, where does this difference really manifest itself? And what is the ultimate self-expression of the penis or vagina in a human being if it can swing so easily between these two extremes of femininity and masculinity? Both qualities exist within every human, so does this mean that the masculine or feminine sides simply swap roles every time a person feels like it?

Language plays an extremely important role in seeing the difference and similarity between man and woman and is the most straightforward tool that allows the full expression of the penis and vagina. Words used by men tend to indicate his strength, power, and control and reflect the gender difference in the declarative, direct, and external statement. On the other hand, a woman's words reflect her diplomacy and shyness, seasoned with a little intricacy and deduction. She uses a language that is similar to her vagina as an internal organ: introverted, mystical, and invisible. And when I say that she is expressing her dissimilarity through language, I mean that she invests in and uses the mental images that she has about herself. Thus, the theory of her distinction as the fairer sex is manifested most in the language through which she expresses herself. According to the GLAAD (Gay & Lesbian Alliance Against Defamation) Media Reference Guide, "Physiological and genetic similarities and differences are not clear sometimes and they cannot indicate the gender really, unless the person introduces him/herself by speech." So the most powerful expression of femininity and masculinity remains speech, or the way that woman expresses her differentiation.

The question now is: what is the image that woman has about herself and how is it reflected through her language? Well, the image she has of herself has undergone countless cultural and historical stages, and throughout this long journey, her mind has been formed through the successive accumulation of said images, primarily by men.

The first image began to take shape from old myths

and has implausible contradictory traits. It contains too many creative, artistic, and magical manifestations and reflects the human being who has two faces and is living within a duality that is apparently very harmonized, coherent, and consistent, and yet remains both clear and vague at the same time. It is the duality of sanctity (prostitution and slavery) and freedom, as well as the duality of life (the giver and the mourner, who is talented in feminine wailing for the dead).

In the old Babylonian creation myth, "Inoma Alish," which goes back to the second millennium BC, there is a clear indication of this duality. The woman here is the only one who gives birth to the creation. The intercourse scene is done in front of the eyes of the isolated male. This makes her "literally and symbolically" in possession of the two poles of existence. She is exactly two in one, just as is the case in any normal act of sexual intercourse. Thus, in the initial ancient texts, the male was excluded in while the female occupied the entire scene.

This "role" did not last long. When metaphysical thought was introduced into the march of human evolution, the need for another type of myth was born as a reaction to this unbalanced duality. The new myth assumed that the male was the one who was here first. However, being lonely all the time, mythologically speaking, made him feel bored and therefore more desirous of seeing his penis, up until now quite passive, involved in more physiological and emotional activities. Thus, human thought entered a new stage and it became necessary, as a turning point in its journey, for woman to adopt other traits and qualifications through which she took into account the hierarchy of power between her and man.

Man was now in need for a companion by a divine decree. "And the Lord God said, It is not good that the man should be alone; I will make him an help meet for him" (Gen. 2:18). "And Adam said, This is now bone of my bones, and flesh of my flesh: she shall be called Woman, because she was taken out of Man." (Gen. 2:23). After that, jurisprudence and legislation were born just for her—a secondary body of law, that is, and not an original one, and there is definitely quite a difference between these two. The original is the purest and from which all subsidiaries come. This fixed body of law is very similar to the legal adjunct; is not a law itself, and therefore woman is not able to draft a decree that fits with the requirements of her mind and her feminine spirit, neither by drawing personal status laws nor by devising a law that reflects her true spiritual and mental nature, unless she knows the essence of her mind and what its needs are. From this point on, a distorted picture of her began to emerge.

Whoever reviews the Old Testament will be

surprised at the numerous mentions of women as though it were simply a collection of anecdotes of evil, adulterous, immoral, and unethical females, some of whom occupied the lives of that era's prophets. The word "woman" is mentioned 782 times in the Old Testament and is used to refer to a "man's female," especially a married one, as well as serve as an analogy for a weak man or a female animal. On the other hand, female names indicate the traits and characters of such women "where the significance of the name was linked and reflecting the condition of the named woman and her character and manner."[12] Isabel, for instance, was the example of evil and her name means "indignity," while Lorhama, the daughter of Joshua the prophet and the harlot Jomir, means "no mercy." Women in this era would carry their fathers' names, like the daughters of Jabeshgilead, Agag, Lot, Job, etc., or take the names of plants and animals such as Tamar (dates), Deborah (Bee) and Zbourah (Sparrow).

Life in old civilizations was filled with all forms of sexual immorality and debauchery—no different from today in which billions are spent on the sex industry for movies, magazines, and other sexual materials. It is interesting that these character-indicating names were common to the period as if they were integral qualities of women. In this old era, the main "job" for a woman was to give birth, which was the most obvious physiological ceiling that was taken into consideration when it came to defining her or introducing her as human being. And this "job" did not offer her any attribute of holiness, really, for motherhood did not cancel out the rest of her "inferior" qualities that the Old Testament talks about. She is false, deceptive, cunning, and jealous and seeks to "hunt" everyone with her beauty if she so desires. Above all, she is a harlot per the definition of the Mosaic Law for adultery. She is just a "loin" that incites a moral collapse. She is also abominated because of her natural "impurity" (menstruation)—a process over which she has no control—tainting everything she touches or even approaches. She is "distinct" from man as she is not allowed to rule or to preside as judge. Her testimony is not accepted and she is denied permission to follow the commandments except those that begin with the words "do not do"(Num. 5:22). She is not permitted to make decisions about her own marriage or be in charge of her dowry. She is in a much lower position where she is treated, to some degree, as if she were a "thing."

Thus, her mind has learned how to survive with minimal loss. She is just a parasite companion and a lichen[13] spirit that quietly grows on rocks and tree trunks.

But where do these traits and characteristics of woman stem from in ancient history? Finding a companion for man was the reason behind the existential and controversial dilemma whose effects are still ongoing.

Initially, the nature of the female mind was thought of as sinful, as if it were an inherent attribute, and the myth of Adam and Eve tells us about the essence of the first female mind and the features of its composition. As a real-life story, it contains broad levels of both reasonableness and absurdity, but dramatically it is still very effective in the popular and spiritual structure of society. This first female mind was the reason for the exodus of the whole of humanity from paradise (according to the biblical version and not the Quran), and thus the first existential problem.

In one of the most important research papers of scholar Hamid Abu Zayd ("A Dialogue Between Religion and Myth"), we find two assumptions for this story. The first one is the "phenomenon" of PMS in women; general pain on the one hand, and the pain associated with pregnancy and childbirth on the other hand. The second assumption is the link that is perpetrated between Eve and the snake. This is not only understood on a figurative level, but also on the level of their involvement together in helping Satan tempt Adam.

In investigating this story, one realizes that the implications are still here to this day, but in a concealed way: PMS is a divine punishment, a bloody, repetitive, penitential, Holocaustic wound that returns month after month to remind her of the same offense. Adam, meanwhile, is seen as the victim of Satan, the snake, and woman. The seduction via the sexual act by Eve came about through eating from the forbidden tree; sex is her ploy, her eternal "trick," to implement her desires and circumvent power and authority. Thus, the first filtering happened automatically: man is the symbol of good—as Abu Zayd argues—and woman is the symbol of evil. Ijtihad[14] has stopped at this point.

While the Quranic text does not throw the responsibility of exodus from paradise on Eve's shoulders, she is still punished, as seduction is forbidden in the biblical references. The Lord said to woman: "I will greatly multiply thy sorrow and thy conception; in sorrow thou shalt bring forth children; and thy desire shall be to thy husband, and he shall rule over thee" (Gen. 3:16), but her major punishment was really her decline from sanity to corruption as a result of committing the seduction act, which caused the incitement of humanity's demise. It is interesting to note that Eve's seduction was originally a stimulus, an event that provoked activity, not merely an event in and of itself to possess knowledge. She was wise before the punishment, so her seduction act was not merely that God of the Bible did not want Adam and Eve to gain knowledge, it was that God wanted them to remain unaware and unself-conscious of their nudity and weakness. Therefore, an in-depth study of this text shows that the revolution, just as creation, was launched from the female mind that has then been punished forever in an endless series of aches and pains. And God did not punish only Eve, but every woman after her.

It is a "punished" female mind, doomed by its own traits and specifications, that continues to survive amid the turmoil of pain that has no end. This is why we find such a large number of evil and unreliable women in these ancient texts, as if their minds, and themselves too, are like undebatable postulates. They are punished with and destined for fragility, tenderness, and pain.

⟨∾⟩∾⟩

In the story of Delilah, about the harlot and the mighty Samson in Gaza, there is evidence of how woman's mind cautiously detours around power and authority in order to survive. Delilah succeeded where others had failed in the defeat of her hero. When the Philistines noticed her love for him, according to the biblical story, they offered her a large bribe to betray him and divulge the secret of his strength. "And the lords of the Philistines came up unto her, and said unto her, entice him, and see wherein his great strength lieth, and by what means we may prevail against him, that we may bind him to afflict him; and we will give thee every one of us eleven hundred pieces of silver." (Judges., 16:5) Thus, her mind began to spin and scheme until Samson revealed the secret that lay in his long hair and then, while he was asleep on her knee (note the body language), she shaved his head, leaving him powerless and humiliated without his strength. This second version of the

Adam and Eve story shows us the hypocrisy and moral collapse that is inherent within Delilah. So while no Philistinian lord could defeat this man's strength with their authority and resourcefulness, the seduction discourse succeeded, and his strength gave way immediately.

Whoever reads this story in the Book of Judges will be surprised by the absence of any warning about the unethical standards of woman's behavior; rather, it is just a passionate, stirring narration about a terrorist who appalled others and ended up as a dead killer. Delilah's mind and her language were praised for putting an end to this legendary hero and she thus secured her survival and the survival of others.

The Arabic legends and myths before Islam did not reach such heights of interpretation of the existence that is signified in ancient Syrian, Mesopotamian, Greek, and even Romanian mythology, nor did they imply such creativity which allows one to ask questions about the concerns of human thought in the face of the challenges imposed upon it. Instead, the concept of woman remained lost amongst stories of veiling, cunning, and sex.

In 1929, Tunisian poet Aboul-Qacem Echebbi delivered an exceptional lecture entitled "The Poetic Imagination of Arabs" at Al Kaldounieh Hall in Tunisia where he talked about pre-Islamic Arabic mythology: "...these myths do not reflect any thought or imagination, and do not represent a manifestation of the universe, or a human emotions; instead, they are simple and naïve monuments like boys' games or girls' dolls, while the rest of the myths do not reveal any deep thought or accurate feeling, and do not symbolize the meaning of noble concepts; rather, they are more illusionary than anything else."

Scheherazade[15] is considered the most steadfast and approved feminine model regarding the role of language as it indicates the sex of the speaker. She is a spokesperson with encyclopedic knowledge and a vast collection of dates, events, and sites that enable her to cover the latent violence with literary flair and verbal excitement. She occupies an echelon more honorable and modern than Eve and Delilah and uses her mind, as much as can be conveyed in that era. She is a celebratory role model of the fairer sex concept who fights murder and violence with courting, passion, and seduction. She also fights the political reality with her own logic or "sexual mind" by perfuming, excessive circumvention, and beautification—i.e. the language of the fairer sex.

This masked rhetoric heads straight to the place in man that does not react to logic or reason: his penis. She uses clever language that fits well with the subject of her "speech." One does not need the intellect to communicate with the body, but rather a way of speaking and terminology that are similar to its level, so she communicates with and via this part of his body. But that's not all; Scheherazade is in the presence of power that is embodied in Shahryar, who no longer needs to feel her through his body, but to know her as well.

She manages, with her own mental capabilities, to call his attention toward "knowing the truth" through feelings and body sensations, inciting in him, again and again, his "sense of excitement and amusement." Thus, she not only speaks the language of his body, but also brings this language to its highest level when she makes the "holder of this body" willing to know.

At this point, I discovered that the idea of a "fairer sex" that is personified by Scheherazade had fulfilled all its dimensions—cultural, sociological, and spiritual—and her mind's components had been shown as a result of a long-term emergency that is required to face her isolation, ostracism, and the immediate replacement by another woman within a space named Haremlik.[16] She had earned her mental weapons with her own strength, motivated by her urge for survival, and became a woman who knows how to defend herself, a woman who is driven and provocative behind a face masked by colorful makeup and jingling trinkets. She is not the same in the presence of power, and her mind is not relaxed enough to reflect on its real features.

She understands that the whole matter is not an amusement, as she is trying to pretend, since her neck could be under the guillotine blade at any moment. Less confidence in herself and her charm, less intelligence, less lying, less decisiveness, or less circumvention could at any moment add her to the contingency of beheaded women, whose charm was not rousing enough to keep them alive in the presence of the power.

It is in the battle for her existence where her binary mind plays its most important role.

Power and circumventing power are extended beyond just dealing with kings, sultans, and caliphs. This power is in every man: every brother, every husband, and every lover. Our memories are inevitably filled with stories of relationships between men and women where observing them is like watching a tennis game; evasion, lying, twisting things around, coyness, disguised seduction or explicit violence are so often evident, as though this natural variance between them was meant to perish them, not help them survive and prosper.

Nevertheless, it is not my intent to simplify the matter, nor to generalize all women's minds, because any discussion about them can't be reduced to only one. Here I am mostly concerned about woman as the eyewitness of her era as well as a partner in crime, about the bitter dreariness of the Haremlik as well as the freedom of lying down under its sun, about the lady in maid's clothing and vice versa, about forbidden passion and the most radical and controlled feelings, about the search for femininity in the office drawers and among the strict, masculine labor laws and the yearning to hide in the cloak of "Mr. Man," about gasping for awards and the desire to isolate herself in the boring family kitchen, about the fear of man and intimidating him, about equality and discrimination, and about frustrating inferiority and the dread of superiority. Finally, it is a matter of fighting legitimate violence and yet secretly chasing after if at the same time.

This discussion can't be reduced to just one woman and does not seek to retaliate but rather see all women as they are integrated with man's morality: those who have attained conscious femininity and those who suffer from a hindered femininity, those who ask for everything from man and those who ask for nothing but his love and respect, those whose spirits have collapsed due to the legitimate mental and emotional violence and those who cannot survive without it. This talk can't be reduced to one woman In the abyss and defending her against all forms of discrimination and violence; however, it is a discourse that encompasses the woman-child, the eternal adolescent, the competitive, the woman of reason, the narcissist, the masochist, the one who seeks security in every move and action, the one who exerts spiritual circumcision on herself, and the one who avoids the scalpel of "ugly education." It is a talk directed to the "every woman," both the women of my country and the women in the rest of the world.

This book is about her, the woman who arises from popular memory, and whom cinematic drama has glorified. She is not a woman who has been "assembled" by an intrigued man, but by another type of man who wanted to chop her head off in the name of love while still pretending that he is her savior. It is a search for the woman who, once upon a time, hovered over the face of the waters with God's word.[17]

It is also research about the woman who is recovered, reconciled with herself, comprehensive, strong, and concealed in the spirit of Thiamt (the female in the myth of creation, Inoma Alish), in the spirit of the hunter of Inkido in the Epic of Gilgamesh, in the spirit of Ishtar, the goddess of love who cursed him and was the cause of his death, in the spirit of Anat who killed Aqhat in the old Canaanite universe, in the spirit of Zenobia, the Queen of Palmyra, in the spirit of the venerable Balkis, the queen of Sheba, in the inspiring wife of the prophet Mohamed Khadija bint Khuwaylid[18], and in Fatima Zahra,[19] Rabia al-Adawiyya,[20] Asmā' bint Abu Bakr,[21] and Khawlah bint al-Azwar.[22]

She is the fragile and weak Faten Hamama[23] who is concealed in the spirit of Al-Khayzuran, the wife of the Abbasid Caliph Al-Mahdi and mother of both Caliph Al-Hadi and Harun al-Rashid, and in the spirit of Madame

Roland,[24] the liberty lady in France, Madame de Staël,[25] the lady of thought, Helen Keller,[26] the anti-violent peaceful spirit who overcomes blindness. She is the strong bustling Sanaa Gamil[27] who is concealed in the spirit of the Virgin Mary and Mary Magdalene.

This is a book about and for all the women throughout the ages.

The Mirror Stage

I discovered the mirror through my mother and my beautiful aunts, and though it could be an ally, I was aware that it was an opponent most of the time.

Every day these women would check out the image that was reflected in the mirrors that hung in their bedrooms, on the entrance walls of their homes, and in the salons. My Aunt Hind was the only one among them to know how deceptive and misleading the mirror was, perhaps because she had a strong connection with her inner spirit and therefore was the most capable of recognizing her true image in that reflection, as opposed to the superficial images supported by her roller coaster of emotions and beliefs.

She used to tell me that the mirror lies most of the time. It is an illusion and we are misleading ourselves when we believe what it tells us. "Your feelings are drawing your reflected image onto the face of your mirror," she would say.

It took me until middle age to discover this reality

and to understand that the image I see is not exactly me. It is a literal reflection of the figure standing before it, as well as a figurative one that registers the intangible details, such as emotion or esteem, in our hormone-driven mirrors.

My Aunt Hind, on the other hand, had an excellent connection with her mirror. Self-confidence was her primary tool that allowed this magical surface to reflect her hairstyle, excessive elegance, and the glamour of her dazzling green eyes. She was luscious and her mirror was the partner in this intriguing, unavoidable lusciousness.

My aunt's healthy relationship with the mirror was considered quite a revolution in her time. In contrast, many times I caught glimpses of my grandmother quickly fixing her eyebrows without a mirror, and in my great aunt's house all the mirrors were covered for seven years after her husband died, for this was the appropriate custom of mourning him. To illustrate how unusual my aunt's attitude was, she once looked out the window to ask her son with whom he was fighting, and was called the ugliest names in return. She was an outcast.

The concept of the mirror was developed over the last century. In my mother's time it was forbidden to look at a woman while she was mourning her husband, then my generation considered the matter obsolete and funny, and now the current generation has completely given up the whole idea of mourning rituals.

When my father died, I resisted the idea of mourning him, but I was forced to do so for what seemed an eternal six months. I knew deep down in my heart that this habit was a worthless, pagan one, which could not return the dead to me and did not mean, at least to me, anything that had to do with honoring him. It had no role in calming my sorrow and distress.

I had to look deeper into the mirror, not as a challenge or self-adoration, but in order to "see" something of my inner self and how time had left its eternal traces on me. The more I looked into the mirror the more I tried to trace my way through this deceptive labyrinth in the "picture" before me. I wasn't able to make the journey to my inner self, not really, nor even truly see my real, external features. My eyes were veiled, obscured, and focused outward on those physical attributes that succeeded in forming this world around me with cunning and malice.

❧

The mirror was involved in this seduction not only in the aesthetic sense, but also in the revolutionary sense that urges, incites, and makes the world disharmonious. It is an indication of woman's comfort with herself and her identity, both literally and metaphorically.

This unique experience of the mirror shows us the strict pictorial value of woman's mental life, for this reflection in the looking glass is neither reality nor an idea. It is, no doubt, a representation of a realistic value, but the reflection is not something material. It is a metaphor in the deepest meaning of the word. That is to say, what the mind sees on its face is only a metaphorical illustration of a material reality, what she believes to be true. More precisely, it is an image of a reality that is seen through another reality. Thus, even the mirror may not allow us to see the true image of reality.

Nature, objects, and other people are just pictures reflected in the mirror of woman mind's which is, in turn, a reflection of this world. The facts and events, metaphorically reflected in the mirror of her mind, are not as they are but as she pictures them. They are symbols of the realities that pass through a sieve in her mind or through her internal and emotionally fragmented life.

The Middle Eastern and East Asian women resting in their Haremlik as displayed in the paintings of Western artists, for example, is the image of woman, or her image as it is in their minds, reflected by the place, religion, and politics of that era. These pictures of woman are similar to her but not exactly her. In contrast, the Arabic female mind grabbed onto those mental images of herself as the unquestionable truth and went from there. What a painful departure, indeed, from reality! It was as if her mind, being suspicious, hesitant, and devout, went right through the mirrors that reflect the facts and realities, passed through fragmented images like an unedited movie, and finally landed on an allegorical image of reality. These likenesses are not thoughts or ideas, nor are they empirical fact. They are what is called the anatomy of metaphor or figurative image.

The figurative image is a suggestion, not a definition nor solid data nor scientific information. It is merely an idea that may, in fact, espouse its opposite meaning at the same time. When conventional language uses metaphor, then, it is yanked up from its roots because the metaphor alters the feeling of the meaning and changes our attitude toward it. Feminine speech sees life as a badly edited movie; that is, she sees it as a series of disconnected pictures around which she must spin in order to make any sense of it. It is the type of communication that uses games and hints to deal with that which is puzzling and elusive, like circumventing authority, and the cultural and moral references quietly disguise the stakes.

Actually, the metaphorical image that woman has about herself has formed the way her mind is able to adapt in general. Oddly enough, the quality of this image has the force to remove the unique ground of her mental life itself and replace it with this fake, figurative one. As soon as conventional language collapses and the flow of metaphor takes over, regular events and facts turn into a creative and artistic experience "where dream lives powerfully in the mind, imagination in the fact, fantasy in the thought, and legend in the meaning," as psychologist Robert Romanychyn states in his book *Mirror and Metaphor*.[28]

The rhetoric of feminine speech is woman's mind's homage to reality, not as it is, but as she feels it is, and as it is reflected in her dishonest and constantly self-augmenting mirror. She is lying in order to tell the truth by developing in herself a sort of innate poetic sensitivity toward the world around her. Woman's mind is her brilliant poetic voice embodied in metaphor. However, it is a sad, clumsy voice and, perhaps, not fully mature. It is a voice based primarily on the cultural platform of "do and do not," on the platform of prohibition and prevention, and on the knowledge that tends to empty the word of its meaning and overwhelm it with hints, puns, politicization, and sanctification. It is a voice nurtured originally on metaphor as an indispensable partner in the structure of this culture.

Now, how does woman see her reflected image in the mirror?

Before answering this huge question, there is an interesting experiment that shows the difference between a human child and a chimpanzee. This experiment is called the theory of the "mirror stage" and is considered one of the most important works of psychologist Jacques Lacan to contribute to the development of psychoanalysis. Lacan saw that the look a six-month-old infant gives to himself in the mirror differs from that of a chimpanzee at the same age. Where the chimpanzee jumps with joy when he recognizes himself in the mirror, the infant runs from it, sensing that this image is an illusion.

The concept of Lacan's mirror stage constitutes an essential understanding of man's recognition of himself. He developed this theory gradually through all his subsequent research until he stopped, in the late 1950s, when he saw it not as a stage in the development of the child, but rather as a stable and permanent awareness of one's recognition of oneself. This period, he argued, is considered one of the stages of growth where human beings become imprisoned by their own image.

Perhaps the Arab woman's mind has stopped completely at this critical juncture of its development because the mirror stage has been observed to be a continuous state of woman's mindset while in the process of building her identity. Rather than one stage, it is a steady and constant process in her growing awareness about herself, and thus she is stuck in this illusion of herself. Moreover, this image has been agreed upon leisurely through passed-down culture and through "the static religious theories which are promoted as the yardstick for knowledge"[29] that

Ibn Taymiyyah[30] considers corruption.

Woman's mind has been shaped over time in the absence of creative freedom and opportunity for comprehension and enlightenment. Its ability to recognize differences, diversities, and similarities has atrophied, and so it has lived for a long time in the shadow of knowledge that presents itself as final, unquestionable, and something that does not need to be reconsidered. Hence, this knowledge has been flooded with distorted images about woman as a species.

With every look at the mirror, she will find her broken and fragmented likeness imprinted on its surface. It is not a reflection of a real image, but a mere fantasy of the real image. She looks at the metaphor of her reflection in the mirror without recognizing herself cheerfully, as the six-month-old chimpanzee is capable of doing. On the contrary, she turns her face away like the six-month-old human infant, for this image is not seen by her in a way that allows her to survive. It is a painful picture, hurtful, and untrue. In addition, since it is purely a metaphor, it carries both its value and worthlessness as fact.

As long as this kind of fixed knowledge is considered Nature's authority, woman's mind learns, through the stages of its evolution, how to circumvent this authority and cultivate it, but always in accordance to the libidinal relation of the mind with its body. Thus, woman is dealing with an authoritarian power and knowledge that is based on the feeling of her body, a feeling that has been rigidly and deeply developed throughout history, unlike its relationship with her mind that stopped its development at the mirror stage.

$$\text{⸘❦⸙}$$

When woman looks into her mirror it is, primarily, to distinguish the identity of her body, the only cultural tool of survival, as a woman. It is decorated, perfumed, and well taken care of. It is glorified, spoiled and is the universe of her existence. Her body has taken on the role of her mind, too—her body being the element of herself that she was able to develop through the ages, as opposed to her mind, which society did not allow her to expand or advance. Therefore, when she looks into the mirror, she sees her body as prominent and superior to any other thing in her world. Furthermore, her care for her body does not follow any decree or restrictions, since she has learned that the hunter (man) and the prey (woman), both must sharpen their weapons and be ready to fight in any given moment.

The excessive growth of her physical "identity" at the expense of her mental "I" leaves her with very little sense of security and an implicit hatred for time. She has learned that her identity remains in the same static state as religious texts and authoritarian knowledge. Consequently, her identity has become blended with the static state of culture, so both are muted in her mind—the very aspect that allowed the physical identity to be formed in such an unprecedented way.

Anyone who watches television is probably not surprised by the quantity of programs designed for and about women. They are situated in prebuilt kitchen studios, fashion show halls, beauty parlors, etc., where they teach women how to properly apply makeup, choose clothes, perfect their body, and keep their man. She plays her "role" in thousands of programs and commercials that are extremely creative about investing certain parts of her body for the benefit of the market and, of course, their sales revenue. Woman excels, too, in the political talk show because her mind is a master of the strategic gambit: her illustrious legacy of the past.

When Lacan developed his theory about the concept of the mirror stage, his focus was more on its structural value and not on its historical worth. To understand woman's mind, we find ourselves obligated to give more attention to the historical value in order to appreciate the essence of the structure. What I mean by the historical is the static history of "knowledge - text - authority," while the structural indicates the eternal conflict and debate between the imagination and the image reflected onto the mirror surface. This stage explains the process of ego formation through the path of recognizing the identity of self, and this recognized self is the end result of this road, worked out by woman with her own virtual image.

⸎

Woman's mind, which stopped developing, figuratively, at the age of six months, is unable to joyfully recognize itself like the chimpanzee does. On the contrary, this mind sees its image through an optical system that lacks coordination and consistency.

The infant sees his image as a whole whose numerous elements that make up this picture give him conflicting feelings due to the deficit of coordination and proportionality in his body, so that, as an infant, he experiences his reflected image as a fragmented and incoherent one. This sense of inconsistency is the first thing to be felt by the infant because the separation is threatening to him as a rival of his own image. Therefore, the mirror stage may heighten an aggressive tension between the infant and his image, as Lacan affirmed.

The same thing happens when a woman looks in the mirror. She knows that this image is hers, i.e. the image of her body identity, but she sees it as quite fragmented, just as an infant of six months sees his own reflection. The conflicting feelings that an infant experiences as a sort of rivalry with his own image is exactly what is taking place in woman's mind. When she looks at her reflected image, she does not see it as similar to the imagined and metaphorical picture that she has about herself. Sometimes she does not even see in this image what is so obvious to others. The insistence of some obese women, for example, on wearing fashions worthy of svelte, young girls is instigated, in my opinion, by the metaphorical image that they have about themselves which is inconsistent with the actual image. As the entirety of the image is threatening to the child, so, too, is it for the woman, and therefore the mirror stage may increase this aggressive tension between the woman's mind and her reflected image.

In order to address this aggressive tension, Lacan says, the infant must associate himself with this image and recognize it as himself. This initial recognition of the identity is what constitutes the "I." Woman's mind must also deal with this aggressive tension by either: 1) ignoring the image and creating another one—which probably already exists in her mind the way she wishes it were, or 2) surrendering to this veiled, age-old conflict between herself and her image.

The recognition of and association with the identity by an infant is considered a moment of ultimate rejoicing, since it permits him to feel his competence and his ability to dominate. His joy is caused by an imaginary victory over, to some degree, his lack of muscular coordination. The joy revelation that the infant experiences may be accompanied by some kind of depressive reaction when, for example, he compares his physical instability with his mother's dexterity and dominance. As for woman, it has been identified that the state of depression that follows the jubilation when she recognizes her image in the mirror is attributable to her difficulty in maintaining this image in a desired shape. The collapse of this desired image may threaten woman's survival and push her, once again, into a hidden struggle with time, man, and herself. She wishes this image, as imagined, to remain polished and ready for any confrontation.

While the child compares his proficiency to his mother's overall ability, the woman's mind has yet another yardstick by which to measure itself, which is man. Because her neurological system is complete and grown, it is normal for her to realize, without conscious thought necessarily, the painful trap of equality that pushes her to keep this image and this dexterity at its best. As time increases man's wisdom and social rank, woman, too, finds herself struggling with time so that she may reap the rewards, i.e. increasing or maintaining her attractiveness.

The mirror stage also has another symbolic dimension. The child turns his head, after recognizing his identity in the mirror, towards an adult in order to receive "approval" of his reflected image. Woman does the same; she turns her head toward a higher ranking in the social and gender hierarchy. She wants others, particularly men or those she considers superior to her, to see her image exactly the same way she sees it. When others do that, she receives her "approval." She is now a certified woman, properly documented and preserved by everyone else.

⚜

When my Aunt Hind used to see me resisting tight outfits, preferring the loose and comfortable ones instead, she would say, "Al-giwa tahid al-kwa," which means "You cannot be gorgeous without some suffering."

Keeping up with beauty is something that requires hard work for sure, but my aunt was right because the returns of being attractive are very high. The doors to paradise are wide open for both women and men who make the grade for society's standard of attractiveness. By the same token, my aunt's political opinions do not differ greatly from her feminine ones. She used to analyze all political events, local and international, and predict the outcome based on the level of handsomeness of the leaders! "I am not sure if President Bush's political deficit was due to the massive destruction caused by his absurd vision in dealing with world issues, or because of an absence of good looks and charisma," as my aunt claimed. I also wondered if her theory was correct about an Arab leader whose neglect by an old ally, the United States government, may have had something to do with his divorce, as she assured me with total confidence! She simply sees things and analyzes them through the filter of her own personal feeling for life, a feeling I started to pay attention to, as it seemed to contain a fair amount of accuracy.

This effort to establish a metaphoric image about the "self" is exhausting, as it opens the door to a more controversial matter, which is narcissism as an inherent feature in the structure of woman's mind. Her reflected image has become an obsession about which she needs constant verification from herself and from others. She wants people to view the beauty and the particularity of her image from the perfect angle and to notice the smallest details, to see the amazing smile that she competently drew on the canvas of her face, to see the lines of kohl that she carefully and artistically smudged around her eyes, to see the outfit that accentuates her well-formed figure. She wants everyone to see her exactly the way she sees herself. This meticulous effort drains her mental and psychological energy and channels it elsewhere, making her less real, less productive, and certainly less happy. It drives her away from life as it is and towards the "instruction" of her lying mirror, which does not know how to reflect the qualities of her inner self nor the vigor of her spirit.

With the spontaneous and instinctive sense of femininity that she has for life, my Aunt Hind never lost sight of the fact that beauty is not enough to attract a man.

"You must make him feel that you are interested in him," she would tell me. "You've got to convince him that you are by his side and working for his favor, washing his feet if he wants you to, making him feel that you are the lady among your friends when you go out together, cooking for him, pampering him and—the most important of all—making him aware that you are faithful to him. At that point, and by doing all that, he will stop caring if you are physically attractive or not. Furthermore, you will get in return what every woman is looking for: real security and freedom."

My aunt's words meant that I should be many women in one—a panoramic and fragmented woman—in order to buy one thing in return: my peace of mind. Her words also indicated that I should avoid being "killed by man's modern sword like Scheherazade," that I must use my wit and cunning to circumvent authority in order to be secure, and that I shouldn't be completely myself (to her, this was total insanity that may result in terminating my life with my own hands).

She also meant that I had to be a "made-up" woman if I wanted to proceed in life without problems or difficulties, for man, as she used to say at the end of every speech, has a child's mind that can be made to give up his weapon by talking to him nicely. In other words, all I needed to do was keep a big thesaurus of complimentary words in my pocket if I wanted to survive. "And what about love?" I asked her. "Well," she said as she looked at me impatiently, "in the early days of marriage, after all, man is a stranger, so one hurtful word out of his mouth will make you hate him. And he is not your son or brother to forgive for insulting you, and nor will he do so. He is a stranger."

Those words were tough to hear for a teenaged girl and a lover, that is to say, someone who did not understand the necessity for Arab women to be like Scheherazade in order to survive. It would be hard for any female whose mind was filled with romantic stories about being drunk in love to hear.

My aunt's speech was about the woman who has something of a narcissistic character, not any other woman. Well, it took me a long time to discover this fact. Actually, she was talking about the Arab woman who "knitted herself up" slowly and thoroughly like a woolen sweater for the sole purpose of becoming a wife.

∝≈

Pierre Daco, a Belgian psychotherapist of last century whose works have contributed to the dissemination of psychoanalysis, has excelled in describing the narcissism of woman, who exaggerates in sharpening the metaphorical and figurative image of herself. He writes:

This [narcissistic] woman plays an important role in

the community. She does not look personal. Her smile is static more often, and difficult to understand. She smiles to everyone the same way, but she is not actually smiling at anyone. [Don't you think that Mona Lisa smile, from the famous Leonardo da Vinci painting, is entirely a narcissistic one?] To her, everything has to be well computed: the way she walks, sits, stands, and the slow way she moves her head and waves her hand that is sometimes marked with indifference. She is the living dead; that is to say, this woman is similar to a chameleon. Narcissistic women, although everyone flocks around them, run away from others by surrounding themselves with mystery that increases their fake charm. She never reveals her true face even in the most spontaneous milieus.[31]

Why does a woman resort to all this? Is it to protect herself from any potential evil? Is it her proactive defense policy? Is it the passion for her own reflected image and her desire to preserve it, even if she pays the price for all the characteristics mentioned above?

This image cannot last forever, at least physiologically. Thus, "the tragic while comes," as Daco says, in which her characteristics become useless. He goes on to state, "The narcissistic woman who feels she no longer catches people's eye is like a dead woman as she senses that this is the stage of excessive make-up, age denial, and anomalous outfits and accessories.... However, her 'care' of herself cannot but make her feel grief and pain, she will mostly fall into a hysterical state with all women who share the same case who are messing around every day in the avenues of forgotten twilight."[32]

The creative description from Daco does not fully explain the comprehensive aspects of the problem of narcissism, for it cannot be considered an inherent facet of the Arabic female mind, but rather a result exactly like any another aspect of her mind. Arab woman is a narcissist only when she is forced to deny her real self in order to survive.

It is true that the art of guile, as ancient texts have long promoted, was an inherited trait as far back as Eve. She had to use circumvention in order to get what she wanted. However, this trait pushed her in an unthinkable direction: she wanted her man to follow the path of knowledge that was divinely forbidden, exactly like Scheherazade who created the daily desire "to know" in the man who used to kill for amusement. The narcissistic mind is characterized by this obsessive investment in one's metaphoric representation against the real and true image.

Psychologist Dr. Robert Emmons[33] considers a narcissistic adult to be far too into himself to have, or even desire, any interest in the common social goals of the community. Staying away from these social goals is usually accompanied by an excessive sense of gender or ethnicity. This explains the withdrawal of the narcissistic woman from any kind of social struggle and why she indulges in her own feelings and the relationship with her partner, which takes up the majority of her mind.

Social struggle is one of the attributes of citizenship in civil societies. This is an "honor" that is offered to the citizen and has to do with public opinion, fame, and social rank. The cultural change of the concept of self-care has rehabilitated the attributes of the narcissist that exist in the structure of her mind so that she starts to engage in some civil non-governmental organizations, not because she likes struggling, but in order to further update this narcissism, and make it consistent and commensurate with the renewable cultural relativism of community to which she belongs.

The female Arabic mind is, by social force, characterized by narcissism, and is mostly veiled. This type of mind is the one my aunt tried to explain to me as an inherent trait in a woman who wants to enjoy security and peace of mind.

In his study entitled "Two Faces of Narcissism," psychologist and researcher Paul Wink states: "A principal components analysis of 6 MMPI narcissism scales resulted in two orthogonal factors, one implying Vulnerability-

Sensitivity and the other Grandiosity-Exhibitionism." He goes on to explain, "Despite this common core, however, Vulnerability-Sensitivity was associated with introversion, defensiveness, anxiety, and vulnerability to life's traumas, whereas Grandiosity-Exhibitionism was related to extraversion, self-assurance, exhibitionism, and aggression." In his study, he discloses that the Vulnerability-Sensitivity type is the result of social disorder and a growing concern of criticism among personal associations, as well as the result of self-abasement. Such a mindset tends to avoid others (especially the partner) because it is a scared mentality or perhaps because it feels–this personality–that it is not eligible for any constructive feelings and emotions of others. The self-abasement and inferiority felt by this type of narcissistic mind prevents the person from acknowledging him/herself. It's a mind, in fact, that avoids diving too deeply into personal relationships and tends to stay away from intimate contact, because this may, she or he thinks, threaten the structure of his or her mind. Wink, in his important study, talks about the difficulty of adapting this kind of mind to any kind of treatment.

❧❧

Delaying the sunset is one of the most exhausting efforts for woman who is trapped at the mirror stage. Her mind, the very thing that does not feel any epistemological stability, finds it difficult to explore its specific cultural foundation and build on it.[34] The fact that the reflected image of self is fragmented is due to the discontinuity found in these thriving cultural and epistemological authorities and not mere fragmentation for the sake of plurality, i.e. the plurality of ways to reach the truth. Woman's mind has become invisible, but it is looking ahead towards change and modernization, seeking a way to link itself to cultures that are more modern and rewarding. Consequently, it enters an unpredictable and turbulent area.

I mentioned in the previous chapter that this mind needs to be aware of its structure and functions in order to be able to draft a law to ensure the highest possible degree of survival. Moreover, I have noted that the concept of law is also ambiguous in Arabic culture, so the resulting disorder is always two-sided: the disorder of the cultural foundation and the disorder in understanding the concept of the law.

This vicious circle is at its harshest and toughest when it is at the childish mirror stage, for the contemporary cultural authority is not fault-free at all, nor is it so pure as to contain only the survival elements of our past illustrious heritage. This culture is contaminated; its sources do not all have the same good quality, and above all, it is supported by audio-visual confirmation, perhaps the strongest evidence of its power being the visual media. This form of media paves the way for a sacred culture to be established in the society because it presents authority in an unquestionable way in its highest hierarchy, so it becomes very absurd and even difficult to get rid of its offered "facts."

The image that remains in the viewer's mind is the one that establishes the mechanism for human effectiveness, and this inadequate information often becomes rooted in memory and builds upon other data in there as well. Missing some essential elements, this data can render the whole collection of thoughts in the mind vague and ungraspable. If a woman is still at the mirror stage, this kind of authority gradually becomes a necessity for her, empties her mind of "content," and configures it per this authority. As Mohammed Al-Jaber, the Arabic thinker, suggests, "rewriting the cultural history with a certain critical approach and under the guidance of our ambitions" is something that may seem somewhat elusive because the availability of an objective criticism or approach is out of the question, at least so far in such a culture.[35]

Criticism or revision in its simplest form is a "method that tends to detect and remove errors, inconsistencies and flaws in theory and practice."[36] By revision, I mean reviewing what is static, handed down or inspiring in our culture, since this forms the largest part of the cultural and inherited body, although this kind of revision is not within the scope of the Arabic mentality at this moment. By criticism I mean that one should formulate the revision questions not on a conceptual level, but based on experimentation, which means that one should be able to build the questions up from personal experiences and suffering and not just by philosophical, abstract tendency.

Furthermore, in-depth criticism and revision allows one to examine and screen things out. This heritage can be not only an obstacle but an integrated body of knowledge as well, regardless of the degree of its confusion and suppression. It seems–this body–to the outside observer as if it has shattered cultural limbs, each one connected to the time and place of its revelation, although this body could, eventually, coalesce into one pot as it is now.

Viewing this body of knowledge figuratively means that we must reconsider it figuratively, too, exactly like anything else the mind may reconsider. However, if this mind is not able to see, in the cultural heritage, an ability to switch direction from time to time and modify the path according to spatial and temporal events, then it is better not to criticize or reconsider it but rather ignore it, and embark upon new foundations that are pertinent to free interaction and to draft new laws that keep the self alive and at the highest possible degree of efficiency and presence.

The female mind that is caught in the mirror stage cannot restore its old ability to interact and deal with the information of contemporary culture. It still sees this world in fragmented images with no real connection between them, therefore, the ability and possibility of critique and reconsidering seem very advanced for a mind that is still in its infancy. In order for woman's mind to critique and reconsider the current cultural reality, it must first come out of the mirror stage and actually look forward with clear eyes and peaceful thoughts. Only after that can the mind examine the components of the culture that made it this way. It has to screen out this culture to choose what is suitable for a distinct feminine entity and only then may it be able to work out its own law and embark from a foundation that is more in tune with its nature.

I hope that this proposal is not just a dream or impossible to carry out, for this mind is apparently still spinning in an orbit that is so different from the other orbits I have illustrated in this chapter. Its path surpasses in complexity the infantile mirror stage, the allegorical vision of self, the shortage in ability to objectively criticize, and the confusion in the face of its heritage. It is the highest orbit of authority, the orbit of the sacred "super-ego,"[37] and the relation to what is divine.

Women Are Mentally Deficient

"Women are mentally deficient" is a sentence that was well-used by some of the men in my family whenever they felt angry at their wives or wanted to make fun of them or tell cynical jokes. Although my grandfather, deep down in his mind and heart, believed in this saying, my aunts managed to go to college and get fully educated without suffering from discrimination, in the strictest sense of the word. Despite that, however, this phrase quickly became a well-used proverb in my family and part of the men's daily "insult dictionary" for whenever they became befuddled by their partners' actions.

Woman is mentally deficient, they believed, because she wants to know about things that are "none of her business," because she argues about everything, because she is jealous, demanding, and interested in the silliest things. She is mentally deficient because she falls in love quickly and is incapable, unlike man, of thinking about long-term plans, instead concerned only about immediate, temporary things. She is mentally deficient because her self-confidence is low and she is only adroit at talking while he excels at "doing" or "being silent." She is mentally deficient because she gets furious for no reason and her tears are always ready at the first emotional jolt. She is made this way because she does not know what she wants and cannot control her tongue or keep a secret. She is also not able to maintain her poise or assume responsibility because of the permanent "agitation" of her hormones and because she is dependent on him even in the upbringing of the children. She is mentally deficient because she cannot manage her finances and is wasteful, always spending money on nonsense, only caring about appearances and neglecting the quintessential and necessary things in life, unlike man.

Woman is mentally deficient and yet he still marries her.

⁓

"Women are mentally deficient" is the most popular Arabic phrase about woman. Despite the fact that the social status of Arab women and the constitutions and laws of Arab societies today seem as if they disregard this low assessment of woman, it is still very much in use.

This "charge," regardless of its origin, is very much an integral part of this metaphoric image that women have of themselves, to the point that a significant proportion of religious women accept it as true and explain it as mere discrimination on the basis of the phenomenon of menstruation as stated in Sahih Al-Bukhari,[38] Sahih Muslim,[39] Jami` at-Tirmidhi,[40] Sunan an-Nasa'I,[41] Sunan Ibn Majah,[42] and other books and Sanads (authentic chain of narrators).

However, before I explain how this statement—and there are many others like it stored in the Arab religious popular memory—has been melded into the structure of the Arabic female mind to become part of the metaphoric image about herself, I want to go back to its origin. This is problematic because this part has become integrated into the accumulated body of knowledge about women without knowing the specific source for most of it. It seems to have reached us through oral frequency or fatwas (a ruling on Islamic law) that made Islam look like a shorthand dictionary for Halal[43] and Haram.[44] These fatwas confirm that the worth of any text is dependent upon the way the text is viewed and read; the more this text is read by a "big mind," the more it is valued and vice versa.

"Women are mentally deficient" is, to many who belong to the school of "accepting passed down beliefs blindly," a sacred statement that should not be touched because it is part of the "Sahih Sunnah." Some Sunni scholars realize that a number of the narrations in the books of Sunnah are al-da'if (weak),[45] al-hasan (good),[46] Al-sahih (complete),[47] Al-marfu',[48] Al-mawdu',[49] Al-mutawatir[50] etc., yet the majority name each narration "Sahih" (genuine or authentic) and forward it with "The Messenger of Allah said..." without examining whether this Hadith is matn or sanad.[51]

Despite the clarity of the Quran in this regard— [Jasiya 45:6] *These are the verses of Allah which We recite to you with the truth; so forsaking Allah and His signs, what will they believe in?* [Aa`raf 7:3] *O mankind, follow what has been sent down to you from your Lord, and do not follow other administrators, abandoning this (the Holy Qur'an); very little do you understand.* [Ankabut 29:50] *Is it not enough for them that We have sent down the Book upon you, which is read to them Indeed in it are mercy and advice for the Muslims,"*—Al-Azhar has issued a fatwa based on Sheikh Muhammad al-Ghazali's statement that considers all narrations in Sunnah books—which include the books of Bukhari, Muslim, at-Tirmidhi, an-Nasa'I, and others—to be established, meaning that one can't build a thought or a judgment on them. Even so, arguments abound about which one should be considered "Sahih Sunnah" among the sixty types of al-Hadith.[52]

The thorough examination of each one of these narrations—those stated in Sunnah and complying with the

WOMEN ARE MENTALLY DEFICIENT

science of Hadith so as to distinguish the accurate from the inaccurate ones, therefore aligning themselves with the Quran—with which Arabic religious culture is saturated will allow us to screen out many of these strange stipulations that have hammered themselves into our epistemological and cultural memory and have attributed themselves to Islam. This is a painful endeavor because if we are looking for "the truth" in the sacred text only that means that looking anywhere else is heresy or atheism.

The public attitude toward this statement about woman is even more appalling when you understand that Islam did not discriminate against people and then judge them accordingly. Islam is commonly understood as a religion of equality and integration: [Ahzab 33:35]*Indeed the Muslim men and the Muslim women, and the believing men and the believing women, and the obedient men and the obedient women, and the truthful men and the truthful women, and the patient men and the patient women, and the humble men and the humble women, and the charitable men and the charitable women, and the fasting men and the fasting women, and the men who guard their chastity and the women who guard their chastity, and the men who profusely remember Allah and the women who profusely remember Allah – for all of them, Allah has kept prepared forgiveness and an immense reward.* [Nahl 16:97]*Whoever does good deeds—whether a male or female—and is a Muslim, We shall sustain him an excellent life, and shall certainly pay them a recompense which befits the best of their deeds.*

In the end, God will not choose a "mentally deficient woman" for an elected task like He did with Mary: [A/I`mran 3:42]*And when the angels said, 'O Maryam! Indeed Allah has chosen you and purified you, and has this day, chosen you among all the women of the world'. Or with Pharaoh's woman that He set her as a good example for all believers.* [Tehreem 66:11]*And Allah illustrates an example of the Muslims—the wife of Firaun; when she prayed, 'My Lord! Build a house for me near You, in Paradise, and deliver me from Firaun and his works, and rescue me from the unjust people.*

The Quran does not blame Eve or consider her responsible for expelling Adam from paradise, so it remains the only correct authority at hand if we ever want to confirm the truth. In any case, we should evaluate the validity and authenticity of the Hadith narrations according to the content of Quran.

When woman's mind is trained little by little and generation after generation to accept this derogatory body of knowledge about her, then we can understand how this mind cannot or may not dare to draft a special law for her own survival. The relationship between the feminine "I" (the female mind) and the existing authority, like everything in the Arab culture, is a relationship of dependency and "non-thinking." In other words, acceptance, receptivity, belief, and obedience.

Authority by definition has to do with values and principles. It is located in a higher position and at a distance from the "I," and contains not only sacred values, provisions, and perspectives, but also the aspirations and ambitions of those who are acting as the representatives of this authority.

The significance of the authority comes from the fact that it plays a pivotal role in structuring public awareness. Actually, it reshapes too many political, moral, and social concepts. If a mind is trapped in the mirror stage, then its relation to authority is very tough and difficult, which has a great effect on this mind. In fact, every time this mind looks at the "I," the self, or to the outside world, it requires approval from this authority. The approval means that the image this mind is assuming about "I" is correct; in other words, the reflected image of self on the mirror needs this authority's approval to reassure its identity in the first place. It's the same with the child who reads his mother's face to determine whether what he saw, felt, and did is right or not. His mind does not care who his mother is, what her education level is, or what her viewpoint is. To him, she is the most powerful being in this scene and the highest position of authority to which he looks.

Although invested in ideology, "Women are mentally deficient" is a statement that can be easily refuted. Throughout the ages, however, it acquired such a sacred meaning that it requires a gigantic effort to dispel it.

Since this statement comes from a religious authority, the confusion is much greater due to the vastness of Islam and the huge variety of its references, many of which are contradictory. This authority has two faces: religious and political. The cleric not only holds the power in his hand, but he is also an intermediary on behalf of the top authority, i.e. God's words, via the sacred texts, which is his job to protect. As long as he is in this position, the jurisprudence of these texts can be re-idealized over and over so as to assume newly defined political dimensions. This dual power has been, historically, associated with the sense of sanctification, and has remained so to a great degree. What has kept this authority in this sacred status is the structure of the mind itself, because this helplessness of the mind makes it possible for this religious, ethical, and political authority to "add fuel to the fire" and feed it with different ideologies so that they are delivered and agreed upon without any debate.

This authority contains not only the lawful body of knowledge, but also the moral one; it provides its information in the form of law in spite of the presumptive certainty of this material, and in spite of the fact that this data is an assumed thought in a continuously variable milieu, coming from a specific period of human history where it may have fit in with the conditions of the time but is no longer relevant.

Since the authority is in position higher than "I" and separate from it, then it is considered somewhere outside of this "I" or outside the cultural structure to which "I" belongs. This explains why "I" recognizes its identity primarily through an outside authority, and not through its own identity and experiences. "I" receives discipline and knowledge from somewhere and someone else who owns the right to govern it and to establish laws and rules that "I" is forced to follow.

Authority that is based on the sacred text does even more: it transforms this holy "truth" into an organization via institutions, scholars, preachers, clerics, and even politicians who use this authority to reshape reality according to their own aspirations. This is what is happening today, for example, with some American neo-Christian politicians or Christian Zionists who are creating a sympathetic atmosphere of the Promised Land for the people. This is an instance of politicization of religion in order to recast reality and create the desired impact (I'm sure that readers have numerous examples in mind in that regard with all that is going on in the Arab world). In short, any debate with this authority is very difficult and requires massive effort to establish its own data with a new approach, because a mind involved in this debate is not only considered incompatible with others' opinions, but also a blasphemer and polytheist.

The Almighty God, being the ultimate authority of this existential inefficiency all around us, is radically different from any other concept of authority we have ever known and is directly linked to the exact and precise natural laws. In addition, God's meaning cannot reflect any discrimination based on gender or species, and it is difficult to frame him or make him subject to any kind of computation process, favoritism, ideology, or restructuring. He is the "Logos."[53]

According to Heraclitus, the pre-Socratic Greek philosopher, Logos refers to all that is holistic and noble. It is the truth in its objective characteristics, i.e. it is an absolute truth located beyond any perceived change or transformation. It provides the link between rational discourse and the world's rational structure.[54] Heraclitus believed that the essence of the human mind emerged from divine essence and that humankind inherently knows the truth through this union, which is considered the most pure and clear mirror in a non-metaphorical sense.

As for Stoics,[55] Logos is the equivalent of the God

concept, the concept of providence and destiny, and is the principle that created the world.[56] It is also what gives humans the power of knowledge and morality. Moreover, Stoics believe that one's mind is part of the collective consciousness, and according to the common divine mind, humans live in harmony with nature where its achievement is most fully shown in the philosopher's mind. Stoics also talk about Logos' duality to distinguish the subconscious mind from the outwardly expressed words; they see that consistency between man and nature is life that is brought about according to the mind and with its permission. This is the leading element in man that indicates our worth as human beings. Consequently, life according to nature is life according to the mind.

When man lives according to the mind, he is not only in harmony with himself but also in harmony with the whole universe, because the mind is not something that belongs only to human beings; it is also one of the characteristics of the universe. To Stoics, the Logos is *anima mundi*,[57] a concept that later inspired Philo of Alexandria, although the content of the term is derived from Plato.[58]

Philo of Alexandria (20 BC – 50 AD) used the term "Logos" to mean an intermediary divine being, or "demiurge."[59] He assumed that the necessity of having those intermediary beings was to bridge the enormous gap between God and the universe.[60] Thus, to Philo, the Logos was the highest of these intermediary beings, and was called "the first-born of God." He also considered that "the Logos of the living God is the bond of everything, holding all things together and binding all the parts, and prevents them from being dissolved and separated."[61]

As for Plotinus, he believed in a totally transcendent "One." This "One" is not an existing thing, nor is it merely the sum of all things, but rather is "prior to all living entities." Being integrated with the concept of God, Plotinus denied that the "One" is sentient or self-aware. The "One" is beyond all attributes of "being and non-being" and is the source of the world—but not through any act of creation, willful or otherwise, since activity cannot be ascribed to the unchangeable, immutable "One."[62] In fact, this quick review about the concept of "word - Logos - God" in Hellenistic Greek thought urges us to pay attention to something extremely important, which is the connection between the idea of God and the mind.

You may notice that God is, outwardly, neutral. He is static and leaves the task of discovering him on the shoulders of humankind. Actually, God has been discovered to be leisurely, as far as the human mind can recognize, and not like the rest of the other traditional "gods." As a concept, God existed before this mind discovered itself. Nevertheless, the concept of God began to develop meaning, little by little, in the first metaphysical perceptions and the paranormal hypotheses of the mystical religions and ancient legends. This is strange because God cannot be realized without the mind, so logically, the mind exists prior to God, or at least it is the tool with which to discover him. In other words, the connection, per the ancient Hellenistic philosophy, between the concept of God and the mind is a very reasonable connection, to a large degree. They are two sides of a single source of authority.

All this started with God as a source for both the known and the unknown. However, God is also seen as an existential, socialist, cognitive, and mystical concept. In fact, he is a "discovery" or, more precisely, he is man's "speculation" on what the essence of God "the omnipotent," "the raison d'être" or the "One" should be. He is not a magician or a totem, but rather a reference to each and everyone, and this reference is associated with the most comprehensive assumption not only for the idea about woman but also for any other concept. Her reflected image on this authority's mirror is *not* metaphorical; she has real proportions. And the reason for this is due to the value of the data contained within the pocket of this reference which is measured by its ability to support man's survival. This rational reference or authority contains natural laws and not arbitrary factors that generate more arbitrary factors every time the mind finds itself facing an explanatory and refuting process.

The purpose of the mind is to solve problems related to survival and it runs the whole structure of the organism in which it exists on the basis of this survival. It does all this out of this great reference, or natural law, that ensures the survival of the species. This instinct to survive is located within the soul, and the very makeup of the body's cells is an immense universal intention (Logos), which is the only stability across all variables. It is the sacred factor that maintains the survival of humankind and the "I."

If woman is to carry out a law that preserves her survival, she has to see her reflected image in the mirror of this first authority. It is a real, non-allegorical image that fits the qualifications of her survival. By doing so, her mind will stop searching hopelessly for this law amongst the lower echelons of these references and authorities.

"Women are mentally deficient" is a presumptive certainty or, more precisely, a consideration. We consider things by picturing them in a particular way so that we can deal with them in a manner that is based on our hypothesis, and as a result, we build our very foundations on mere consideration.

The concept of "consideration" in this sense is located in a higher place than the mechanism by which the components of the universe (matter, space, energy, and time) move accordingly. "Consideration" has the power and strength to recast or reshape matter or the supposedly solid viewpoint. In other words, the thought or idea, which is a consideration and an assumption, is higher in ranking than the matter itself. These elements (matter, space, energy, and time) are themselves collectively agreed upon considerations at a broad level, and thus they are the products generated by these considerations or assumptions that life approves on an eternal basis.

When the human mind accepts any consideration or assumption as an absolute certainty, it turns it into a solid, existing truth by mutual agreement. In order for an agreement to occur, it not only has to be issued by an authority that is derived from an even higher one, but it must also have the appearance of irreversible determinism.

Ideas are not less important than matter, space, time, and energy; on the contrary, they give those elements their stability, solidity, and existence by permanent agreement and approval. In fact, the test of an individual's freedom lies in his ability to change his assumptions and considerations that have to do with the physical universe, the life around him, and his role in all this.

These degrading statements about women have unconsciously messed with the function of her mind and forced some mental behaviors to show up as an inherent part of her natural beingness. Her mind, as we recognize it now, is self-determined, as opposed to what religious authorities expect and request from her. Her mind's self-determinism stems from the desire to control all existing elements of her survival and is no longer willing to fall into the trap of painful possibilities. Her long history of imprisonment in the religious, political, and social Haremlik did not leave any option for her to allow her own destiny to be played out because any uncalculated, small mistakes may have threatened or completely eradicated her existence.

Today, because she has become a working human being at a very broad level, she wants to invest in herself more than ever, even to the point of obsession. To her, this is her only opportunity to take revenge for the long, agonizing history through which she suffered, and her mind's task from this point on seeks to erase all traces of this painful journey with the little amount of energy that she has left. Her mind does not even look into the first authority's mirror—God—where she can see her pure and non-metaphorical image that is in accordance with the natural laws so as to ensure her survival in the best possible way. How could she, when her mind never learned how to build a factual and transparent bridge to the first authority? Instead, she preserved her relationship to authorities and references that are "far away" from her, outside her "I," and always according to the approved religious and social "folklore." Her mind does not see time, reality or the physical universe as they are, but instead sees them as "things" that she craves in moments of pain, frustration or joy in order to ask for help or to thank. In this way, she categorizes or classifies this authority and gives it characteristics instead of realizing it as the character itself. God's mirror is much larger, deeper, and more important than any other mirror at all, because the observer will not see the qualities in this reflection as separate and fragmented, but as a divine and conscious unity, for this authority is the essence of the quality itself. This authority is not only wise but is wisdom itself. It is not only capable but is capability itself.

When woman's mind begins to use God's mirror as an alternative to the second-tier authority, which is overloaded with endless fatwas and justifications and details, she takes her first step toward identifying her true nature. Unfortunately, few women use this mirror to look at themselves. The ones who do are not necessarily religious, for this is not a mandatory condition to establish a relationship with God. Many people who are able to find their way in this life depend on the very characteristics and human qualities that God granted them with no shame.

Self-determinism is not the only peculiarity by which woman's mind is characterized; it is also driven by fear, which is the result of a mind that does not know how to see itself in the mirror of the first authority. Fear as an inherent characteristic in the structure of woman's mind is the same fear that is installed in the Arabic mind in general.

It is interesting, for instance, to read what Ibn Khaldun[63] wrote in a chapter entitled "Sorcery and Talismans" in Part VI of his book *The Muqaddimah* (or *Prolegomenon*). He defined these two words as "sciences showing how human souls may become prepared to exercise an influence upon the world of the elements, either without any aid or with the aid of celestial matters. The first kind is sorcery. The second kind is talismans." Sorcery and all its heresies, so widespread in Ibn Khaldun's era, originally existed to circumvent the forces that we cannot control with a human's standard of physical and mental powers. Sorcery was invented by a fearful man and is one of the features of Eastern people, the backbone of all ancient civilizations.

Khaldun talked about the degrees of mystical souls. He believed that they are not rational and are "directing oneself to the spheres, the stars, the higher worlds, or to the devils by means of various kinds of veneration and worship and submissiveness and humiliation. Thus, magical exercise is devotion and adoration directed to (beings) other than

God. Such devotion is unbelief."[64]

Furthermore, he could also see that "among the Sufis, some who are favored by acts of divine grace are also able to exercise an influence upon worldly conditions." Khaldun indicated that the ultimate purpose of sorcery is to change the elements and nature's forces by mental dynamism and not by any artificial means. This isn't a current reality, not only because of the human deficit, but also because of the depth of fear that exists within us. Although fear has been common in the human race from day one, its traces remain in the Arab mind because the Arabic culture and the era in which Khaldun lived are referred to as "ages where the transmitted word and narration dominated." Ibn Khaldun believed that the critic and the mind come before transmission and narration. The revolution that he created in the human thought in general has to do with his real experience and consulting rationality that takes precedence for him and not only the theoretical approach."[65]

The allocation of these chapters on sorcery, divine powers, logic, mental sciences, and medicine in his *Prolegomenon* is an another attempt to run away from transmission and metaphysical culture to the other side of the river, which is logic and rationality, in order to go back and see the self in the mirror of the first authority. Perhaps Khaldun realized that "the preoccupation of life after death instead of this real, existing life is the biggest hindrance to modernity. However, this did not happen, though if it has happened, the Muslim community won't omit the industrial leap that has put end to all discussion and settle the matter in favor of the West."[66]

⚜

The mind that finds it easy to transmit or recount any narration without thought or rational judgment is a fearful mind. With few exceptions, Arabs are characterized by this "trait" as inherited in the structure of their minds. Perhaps the best approach in understanding this issue is in Ibn Khaldun's amazing diagnosis in his *Muqaddimah*, not only of the Arab culture but also of the general state of mind back in its early formation. He stresses that the mind should have the ability to differentiate, i.e. override the mirror's image of self or "I" as fragmented and unclear. Since Khaldun is an evolutionist, as described by Tunisian thinker Mohamed Altalibi, he separates man from animal, knowing that the ability to think is what distinguishes the two species and makes him feel his pure humanity.

He says in his *Muqaddimah*:

> God distinguished man from all the other animals by an ability to think which He made the beginning of human perfection and the end of

man's noble superiority over existing things. This comes about as follows: Perception—that is, consciousness on the part of the person who perceives of things that are outside his essence—is something peculiar to living beings to the exclusion of all other existing things. Living beings may obtain consciousness of things that are outside their essence through the external senses God has given them, that is, the senses of hearing, vision, smell, taste, and touch. Man has this advantage over other beings. It is the result of special powers placed in the cavities of his brain. With the help of these powers, man takes the pictures of the sensibilia, applies his mind to them, and thus abstracts from them other pictures. The ability to think is the occupation with pictures that are beyond sense perception, and the application of the mind to them for analysis and synthesis.

The ability to think has several degrees. The first degree is man's intellectual understanding of the things that exist in the outside world in a natural or arbitrary order, so that he may try to arrange them with the help of his own power. This kind of thinking mostly consists of perceptions. It is the discerning intellect, with the help of which man obtains the things that are useful for him and his livelihood, and repels the things that are harmful to him.

The second degree is the ability to think which provides man with the ideas and the behavior needed in dealing with his fellow men and in leading them. It mostly conveys apperceptions, which are obtained one by one through experience, until they have become really useful. This is called the experimental intellect.

The third degree is the ability to think which provides the knowledge, or hypothetical knowledge, of an object beyond sense perception without any practical activity (going with it). This is the speculative intellect. It consists of both perceptions and apperceptions. They are arranged according to a special order, following special conditions, and thus provide some other knowledge of the same kind, that is, either perceptive or appreciative. Then, they are combined with something else, and again provide some other knowledge. The end of the process is to be provided with the perception of existence as it is, with its various genera, differences, reasons, and causes. By thinking about these things, man achieves perfection in his reality and becomes pure intellect and perceptive soul. This is the meaning of human reality.[67]

Based on the above, man is not only able to recognize the outside world through his senses, but also perceive the emotion that comes with this recognition. The mind, which distinguishes itself in the mirror from anyone else, is aware of its uniqueness and individuality. This mind is not subject to sorcery because it is afraid of something, and does not attempt to predict the future due to laziness, but rather depends upon thought that allows it to discriminate, perceive, intuit, and induce. What Ibn Khaldun said 600 years ago is still valid to this day. He has exceeded even the concept of Logos itself, and avoids the bashing of Hellenic thought to say that the truth is just there in "the belly of the mind."

Women have inherited fear as part of the overall structure of the Arab mind. The practice of reading one's fortune in the coffee grounds of an upside-down cup in Arab houses is neither usual nor insignificant. It involves, in large part, a metaphysical and cabalistic concept, albeit in its simplest sense, where we find a plethora of phobias at the bottom of the coffee cup. This is much more popular among women than men.

Although conjuration (invoking a sacred name) has almost disappeared in some civilized and educated societies, the upside-down cup myth has, to our surprise, remained widespread amongst highly-educated women. In fact, they surrender to an illiterate cup reader even while knowing that their fortune does not involve any proven fact. This is actually a situation where the educated woman feels very relaxed because she has an opportunity to stop her mind from analyzing and manipulating, and instead reassure herself of her happiness and survival.

It is remarkable that these phenomena have not disappeared from society despite all the scientific and technical progress we've made and in spite of the increase in woman's personal awareness. On the contrary, these metaphysical phenomena have taken more sophisticated forms, thanks to technology, and electronic astrology is a good example of this.

The close observation of these phenomena reveal that they are not disappearing with scientific and cultural progress because their endurance has to do with something else completely. Fearful minds that seek their security in divination, sorcery, astrology, and upside-down coffee cups are paralyzed by frustration—a constant epidemic in our Arab world. This feeling derives from widespread poverty and everlasting economic malaise, from the high cost of living and poor education, from the disregarding of women and the nastiness of legitimate violence against her, from the absence of civil government where the constitution is based on human rights, from the deficiency of social justice, from the failure of national policies, and from the neglect of the individual that is being prosecuted.

All this creates a kind of public frustration, weighing on the individual, especially woman, by pushing her into fear and neither acknowledging nor granting her responsibilities. Is it any wonder that she seeks and enjoys this kind of metaphysical and mystical relaxation in the coffee-cup fortune telling?

If you observed the phenomena of sorcery and superstition in the Arab world, you would be amazed at how many charlatans exist and the billions spent on this type of business.

At the bottom of the coffee cup, not only do we find an escape from responsibility and the temporary avoidance of personal problems, such as spinsterhood, divorce, failure in love, infertility, marital disputes, self-abasement, and loneliness, but also certain forms of phobia. I have distinguished five basic types of phobias of Arab women in the "scum" of the reversed cup. These fears are behind the attraction to metaphysical activities, sorcery, divination, and fortune telling, and I think that examining and explaining them will shed more light onto the curious structure of this mind.

This image of the reversed coffee cup left aside to dry in my grandfather's house, and other houses in the neighborhood, has been familiar to me my whole life.

Although my aunts and grandmother did not believe in these "dreamed up stories" one hundred percent, it was nonetheless relaxing for them and made them breathe a sigh of relief to "remove a huge rock standing over their chest," as they used to say, even for a few minutes. They were skillful at creating a colorful world of femininity, a world that was bright and full of emotions, coddling words, and cries of concern, and were willing to bear the permanent knocking at the doors from neighbors, friends, and relatives for the pleasure of a quick coffee and upside-down cup reading. Life becomes very small when feminine tenderness and fear coexist in a melting pot of our sad existence.

Once more, I ask: can "Logos" be the first authority?

Appendix of the Meaning of Logos in Christianity and Sufism

Christian theologians often consider John 1:1 to be a central text in their belief that Jesus is God, in connection with the idea that the Father, the Son, and the Holy Spirit are equals. However, only in this verse is Jesus referred to as the Word of God, the theme transposed throughout the Gospel of John with variations.[68]

In fact, it is imperative to differentiate between the meaning and the translation of Logos, as rendered by the various traditions and texts. Gordon Haddon Clark, the

American philosopher and Calvinist theologian and the expert in ancient philosophy before Socrates, has defined the Logos as "logic." He wrote, "The well-known prologue to John's Gospel may be paraphrased, 'In the beginning was Logic, and Logic was with God, and Logic was God.... In logic was life and the life was the light of men." [69]

Actually, Clark was alluding to the idea that the "laws of logic" are contained in the Bible itself, thus they were not a secular principal imposed on the Christian vision of the world. In the Gospel of John, for example, we realized that Philo of Alexandria's logo concept was adopted referring to Christ as the embodiment of the divine logo who created the universe and shape it.[70]

On April 1, 2005, Joseph Cardinal Ratzinger (who became Pope Benedict XVI two weeks later), delivered a lecture in the convent of Saint Scholastica in Subiaco, Italy, upon reception of the St. Benedict Award for the promotion of life and the family in Europe. In his speech, he pointed out that Christianity is the religion of the Logos:

> Christianity must always remember that it is the religion of the logos. It is a faith in the Creator Spiritus, the source of all reality. This faith ought to energize Christianity philosophically in our day, since the problem we now face is whether the world comes from the irrational, and reason is therefore

nothing but a 'byproduct,' and perhaps a harmful one, of its development—or whether the world comes from reason, so that reason is the world's criterion and aim.... We Christians have to take special care to remain faithful to this basic principle: we have to live a faith that comes from the logos, from creative reason, and that is therefore open to all that is truly rational.[71]

In his important book *Sufism: Love and Wisdom*, Roger Gaetani explains the concept of Logos in Sufism.[72] He gives the word an even broader horizon and connotation to mean the relation that links the "Uncreated" (God) to the "Created" (man). As for a Sufi deist, a Logos is the connection between man and God. This is a fascinating thought because it makes man an organic, integral part of the authority itself and the logos as a "link" that might lose its essence without the presence of man. Even God as an authority consequently becomes inaccessible and unreachable and his existence loses the utmost meaning.

Even Ibn Arabi[73] might have assumed the concept of Logos from Neo-platonic and Christian sources. He is assured that the Logos or "Universal Man"[74] is a mediating link between human beings and the divine essence.[75]

Sufism in that meaning is a universal path, although it is not my objective here to examine the structure of each religion and belief since what concerns me the most is the workability and the application, and how this can affect the authority that woman's mind is dealing with.

The Five Fears of the Female Mind

Fear was quite apparent in the behavior of the women in my family. Even with the relatively little freedom they had, still more taboos were imposed upon them, so they learned to either avoid these restricted activities or subjects, or approach them carefully. I didn't pay much attention to this at that stage of my life.

The spiritual and moral life of woman has evolved, ostensibly, at the same rate as technological development (at least in Syria), contrary to what has been thought. However, this speed may have been superficial, unreal, and inaccurate, because it hasn't helped the female mind get rid of these fears. I, myself, am paying the price for the discrimination that my mother and grandmother endured, because my mind suffers from post-traumatic stress disorder.

This freedom that has been available to me, because of the political resolution that endorsed the empowerment of women in Syria, has allowed me to calm down a bit, reconsider things in my mind, and keep myself at a certain distance from what was/is happening. Some freedoms which were not allowed even in my mother's generation were accessible to me and my generation because they were expected from and granted by society. Nevertheless, the remnant of fear was still instilled in the structure of my mind and the mind of many women, regardless of their environment and their upbringing.

Going to the movie theater or to the beauty salon or even chewing a gum in public were signs of idleness and deterioration to my grandfather. On the contrary, my highly-educated father used to let me violate all those rules without question. Seeing my mom and aunts wearing immodest dresses, my grandfather would become furious, while my father's reaction was much more indifferent; he might turn a blind eye, or simply whisper to my mom, "Her dress doesn't fit her well. Ask her to change it if possible."

Even though my father worried about me, he still respected, to a large degree, my right to freedom, allowing me to travel anywhere, especially if education was the reason behind my departure. He believed in empowering women, albeit with some caution, since this historical fear was a part of his mind, too.

The times have changed, but this fear remains, because it is the voice of my grandfather, and not my father, that is most audible in my ear. Perhaps this shift in personal freedom that women have experienced in some Arabic countries, including Syria, is due to a political resolution and not to her spiritual needs or the evolution of these needs through time. In fact, like all resolutions in our Arab world, this resolution has "descended" from "above" rather than been brought about because of the individual's struggle with her ideological and physical leanings.

In order to explain what I mean by this, I must add that I am not talking about the sick female mind, nor do I wish to generalize all Arabic female minds with prejudiced statements about their mental structure by calling them "deficient." On the contrary, I am talking about a collective Arabic female mind within the context of its historical development up to the present day: the fears that have been instilled in her mind through the ages by cultural, spiritual, and folkloric shocks.

If we agree that the Arabic woman has been through unprecedented periods of repression, hardship, and disregard, then we must agree that her mind today is living in a post-traumatic stress state while trying to coexist with the world around it by using what is left of its abilities. The relationship between cause and disease or between the incident and the consequence (fear) is not just coincidence, but rather the former serves to prime the latter.

Arab woman was exposed to incidents where her survival was literally threatened, and these incidents have left, quite inevitably, an impact on her mind and behavior. Thus, she will naturally and unconsciously tend to avoid all future possibilities of these types of incidents. If being ignored or insulated, for instance, happens often enough, then a permanent, subconscious fear will take up residence in her mind about these things. The structure of the mind is such that it will react to these fears even though they are not a current threat.

In this chapter, I want to shed some light on post-traumatic stress disorder, as well as on these five fears, which have been stored in the mind as a result to her long history of suffering. I also want to examine the effects of these oppressive shocks and confront them, if possible.

Communities that are exposed to disasters and wars are more prone to the spread of disease among their members. These difficult periods may create irreversible effects within the individuals, such as obsessions, fears or phobias, self-harm, depression, and anxiety or panic attacks.

Beyond all other effects, fear is the most powerful and threatening feature that leaves its thumbprint on the structure of the mind. Fear as a result of trauma does not necessarily mean that woman's mind is afraid of everything. What happens in circumstances like war or disaster is that she may develop phobias about specific things that stay in her mind and coincide with social norms, or religious and cultural taboos that her mind was forced to confront and deal with over time.

Often, these fears may not be justified in the present moment, but they manifest themselves because of a compelling desire to avoid certain things that she finds her mind dealing with; these fears and obsessions are attempts at a proactive defense. This is another reason that reveals this mental structure to be self-determined: her mind knows that this fear may not be in proportion to the level of the expected or perceived danger, yet it is unable to control the matter or explain it.

Remarkably, it is difficult to expect such fears to disappear from the caves of her mind whenever she finds itself in a different environment because of the accumulation and nature of the shocks. Any new shock will trigger all psychological manifestations related to the previous shocks and make her live them out quite painfully. However, understanding the circumstances of the socio-cultural, political, economic, and epistemological incidents, and looking at them as general, rather than personal, misunderstandings or tragedies, would restore some of the security to her mind and thereby allow it to relax and become less fragmented.

Although I have traveled around the world frequently, I could not change much as a woman. I have lived in environments that are quite liberal and open, yet my lifestyle and habits stayed almost the same. At first it took a tremendous effort on my part to take my laptop to a coffee shop in Los Angeles, for example, and hide out in a quiet corner to write because I thought that everyone was looking at me. However, after very little attention from those around me, I realized that everyone else was engaged in their own activities or thoughts. I relaxed then, but I couldn't help thinking about all these "small freedoms" that women continue to struggle for in some Arab countries. Though the environment around me has changed, the cumulative shocks have kept me alert and motivated. And though my grandfather and father have both died, their words still echo throughout the house. Sometimes I feel inexplicably afraid, but other times I reflect on my father's indifference about these rules for women, so I proceed with my life and try to remember that he is the one who trusted me and "offered" me my freedom.

The severe contradictions in Arab society make it difficult to deal with the problems of reality in a systematic and thoughtful way, instead forcing people to resort to enthusiastic and undebatable ideas that allow them to see things as hypotheses without results. This is the main fact that the Arab female mind has to understand in order to start her first step to healing.

Long-term violence, both moral and physical,

against the Arab woman is beyond her nervous system to handle. It is a repetitive violence that has exerted tremendous pressure on her through the ages so that, in order to deal with it, she has been forced to create her own defensive means and tools, such as obliviousness, avoidance, and escape, either physically or emotionally.

The degrading image of women throughout history has changed her idea about herself and about the whole world and made her suffer from this jumble of fears, which have become, over time, an integral part of the structure of her mind. At the same time, focusing on the strength of man and his superiority has made it impossible for her to even see herself as an vital part of this world. Ultimately, the violence that has been directed towards her for so long has resulted in the same deep-seeded, general, and overriding fear created by the news media about the so-called dangerous environment in which we live. The repetition of these degrading images about woman has crippled her and made the mere idea of searching for her true self unthinkable.

❧

It is interesting that fear (and phobias) is more prevalent among women than men, especially *the fear of being alone* or staying single. This kind of fear is the result of a lifetime of shocks of the same content. Isolating woman throughout history, either literally in the Haremlik or more covertly by being excluded from participating in important community activities due to cultural and religious tenets, and then reinforcing this isolation through masculine labor laws, has created in her a rigid sense that she is "alone," "left behind," and "forgotten," just because she has a fragile physical structure, and so-called "deficient mental abilities." Furthermore, her physical structure—her body—is perceived as dangerous to her community: it is misleading, seductive, and stimulates corruption. She is neither part of life's movement nor a partner of its vitality, but a mere uterus motivated by the fluctuation of nature, hormones, and uncontrolled emotions.

The fear of being alone or single tends to be a chronic fear, which evolves and manifests itself only when anxiety develops as a result of attempting to avoid that very fear. It is true that the immediate reason for any fear may be unknown, but psychology tells us that the cause is often due to something that has been repressed or dissociated from, such as brutal emotional or physical trauma experienced in the individual's past. On the other hand, the researchers and scientists of human behavior see that these fears are only responses by which the individual is trying to avoid a certain situation or attitude that is the subject of his/her fear and concern.

It is remarkable that if you routinely avoid the

subject of your fear or phobia, over time you may lose your self-esteem and feel weak, cowardly, and inefficient (which are the traits that women are accused of in general). If you cannot control your fears and instead try to avoid them, you may feel some sort of depression of moderate intensity that makes you resort to alcohol, drugs, obsessive shopping, compulsive sex, or any other addiction in order to numb the pain of avoidance. I won't go into details about addictions, as there are many other terrific books that cover that. My intention here is to understand the nature of the fear of being alone and single, as well as its impact on the behavior and mental structure of the Arab woman.

With time, a part of the female mind learned how to coexist with the image of herself in society and other people's mirrors, and to accept her inferiority. But at the same time, the other part of her mind tried deliberately to avoid the whole matter by resisting this image and staying away from anything that might preserve the painful experiences that occurred repeatedly over the course of her life. And so it is a constant struggle for her whether to accept this image of herself or not.

Woman is alone when infertile, divorced, unmarried, elderly, or when she is considered unattractive. She is alone, too, when she initiates love or talks about her private life, because others instantly categorize her, judge her, and lock her up in an isolated room, emotionally or socially speaking, when she doesn't hesitate to be herself. She is asked to show her false perfection and be socially acceptable, while no one acknowledges her true self.

Let us take the example of an unmarried young woman. In observing her behavior and the complicated way she deals with life around her, we see that she is someone who suffers, due to the depth of her fear, sometimes conscious, sometimes subconscious, from compulsive obsessions such as being a neat freak or anorexic, as if these fixations could smooth out her doubts or allow her to avoid unknown dangers and the uncomfortable feelings around them.

We hear a lot about unmarried women who are superb at organization to the point of exhibiting Obsessive-Compulsive Disorder (OCD). We find these women everywhere, as managers, executives, and administrators, who are brilliant at running businesses, offices, and households, but are slaughtered by emotional insecurity that weighs on them so heavily that they try to make up for it by compulsive and unjustified actions and practices. They organize everything non-stop and for hours at a time. What makes them act this way is the aching fear of strenuous loneliness that urges them to soothe it by any means possible! This need for fanatical organizing is due to a deep depression and the inability to see the creative abundance of life.

The artistic nature of woman cannot easily cope with the strict made-up laws because she tends naturally to express herself in spontaneous and emotional ways, and to give her personal touch on the environment around her. Nevertheless, when we see her diving into her own obsessive calculations, we must realize that she may be a depressed, lonely, and pitiful woman. (Note: obviously some women are organized because they enjoy it, but it is the obsessiveness around it that we are discussing here.) Above all, there is no moral aspect to these obsessive and excessive behavioral tendencies, because her real spirit is usually absent in these moments. She is a lonely woman trying to fill the vacuum of her soul by returning these scattered things to their places like a machine unaware of what she is doing.

⁓

The second of the major fears that characterizes the Arab woman's mental structure is *the fear of being buried alive,* or taphophobia. Psychological and medical dictionaries explain this kind of fear as "a fear of being placed in a grave while still alive as a result of being incorrectly pronounced dead."[76] Believe it or not, history is full of incidents of people being buried alive after mistakenly thought of as dead because medicine was not as accurate back then as it is today, so you can see that this type of fear was quite justified. However, this matter is not one of my concerns in this book. The type of fear that I am most concerned about, that I found inherited in woman's mental structure, is the one that is brought about by old, accumulated incidents wherein she was intentionally buried alive while she was still a newborn—just because she was female and might cause shame and disgrace to the family and the tribe.

History tells us the story of infanticide with more details. Dr. Larry Milner talks about this issue in his important book that is the result of ten years worth of research, historical studies, and recent data, and is an intensive scientific investigation on the proportional number of children who have been killed at the hands of their loved ones. Milner has established that "the ability to easily terminate a pregnancy, and thereby terminate an unwanted child before it is born, has had a profound effect on the prevalence of infanticide...the human species has killed almost 10-15% of all children born in the time that Homo Sapiens have evolved."[77] When we go back in time, we find out that this type of murder was widespread among ancient and underdeveloped communities and tribes as well as among the modern and civilized ones. Infanticide, which is defined as killing a child within a year of birth, was practiced on every continent around the globe and by people from different cultural and educational levels, from agriculture communities to the most advanced civilizations.

Milner discovered that the unreasonable tendency of parents to kill their children was developed under the pressure of a certain combination of difficult situations. In nineteenth-century England, for example, infanticide was impressively widespread, so a huge argument was raised in the medical and scientific milieus about how to control and resolve it. In spite of the diversity of causes that are behind the infanticide phenomenon, we can statistically monitor two important factors that are involved in this matter: poverty, and the desire to control procreation. Since the dawn of history, obtaining food has been threatened by the increase in population, and infanticide was a way to control this so that people could avoid the potential effects of famine.

Charles Darwin, English naturalist and writer and best known for his theory of evolution by natural selection, has postulated that killing children, especially girls, "was the most important suppressor facing the increase of population in early times." Why was the death of female infants so necessary for the survival of the tribe? Does this survival have anything to do with securing food? Or was survival merely camouflage for the discrimination against females? Alternatively, was there something else going on, such as the archaic concept of honor and shame where killing female newborns was the way to "calm" the tribe's worries for any potential future shame? A prevalent saying at the time, which was one of the popular unofficial laws in force, was: "It is a matter of magnanimity and nobility to bury an infant female."

Islam prohibited the killing of female infants, as it was a crime taken as seriously as any other murder.[78] However, this attitude has not abolished the discrimination, which seems to go back to something deeper and more complex in the structure of ancient societies. The pre-Islamic Persian Empire was a patriarchal society where the female was considered an undesirable hell for a family struggling to survive. Although infanticide was known to the Arab tribes before Islam, too many reasons were behind this crime. Some people have justified infanticide for reasons of integrity and morality, or from fear that a girl may be kidnapped by enemies during a war or invasion, for which shame would most certainly be brought to the tribe. Still others used to kill their newborn females who were born with disabilities or deformities, another indication that woman's worth is in direct connection to her physical beauty and nothing else.

In Judaism and Christianity, the prohibition of murder is stated right there in the Ten Commandments: "You shall not murder." However, it is not as simple as that because woman has always been considered the property of man: "You shall not covet your neighbor's house. You shall not covet your neighbor's wife, or his male or female servant, his ox or donkey, or anything that belongs to your neighbor."[79]

Woman was also sold: "If a man sells his daughter as a female slave, she is not to go free as the male slaves do,"[80] and this is regardless of her age. Above all, Jewish woman was not allowed to stand up for herself in court and give her statement, so her father was the one to represent her in all legal matters. A Jewish man could also offer his daughter as a sacrifice or guarantee under the so-called sacred prostitution or sacred sex ritual.[81] Thus, the commandment "You shall not murder" seems senseless when compared to woman's degrading status. Furthermore, the Old Testament is filled with endless evidence of her low position, starting with blaming her for the first sin (Judaism and Christianity both jump on that band wagon) and ending with trading her in the goods market. The only reason she has been called a "saint" is because she occupies a prominent place in the temple as a "sacred prostitute." She is born in unrighteousness—"Behold, I was born in guilt, in sin my mother conceived me"[82]—so therefore she deserves to be killed! Jewish jurisprudence is built entirely on the basis that woman had been born sinful, so the commandment "You shall not murder" may exclude her.

Though Judaism is the religion out of which Christianity was born, the latter religion separated itself from the former and did not build its structure on the

Jewish doctrine in which there is a clear discrimination between man and woman as well as between Jewish and non-Jewish. To a certain extent, Christianity has a different perception for women.

When an adulterous woman was stoned to death in Judaism, Jesus would not condemn her, instead saying to those who did, "Let any one of you who is without sin be the first to throw a stone at her."[83] The leaders of Israel put God to the test by way of his Son, repeating the Israelites' historical pattern on more than one occasion in the wilderness at Meribah and Massah.[84]

While seated, Jesus bent over and wrote with his finger in the sand without looking at the woman or the crowd around him. This act of writing on the ground is itself very significant. Kenneth E. Bailey points out that it was unlawful to write even two letters on the Sabbath, but that writing with dust was permissible (Mishnah Shabbat 7:2; 12:5). If this were the eighth day of the feast, which was to be kept as a day of rest, then Jesus' writing on the ground would show that he knew not only the law but also the interpretations of it.[85]

Therefore, killing the female newborn is an "ongoing event" from birth until the day of her death (unless she dies naturally) within a socially acceptable discriminatory system. After the Babylonian captivity, Jews were grateful to God that they had not been born Gentiles, slaves, or women: "Blessed are You, O Lord, King of the Universe, who have not made me a heathen. Blessed are you who have not made me a bondsman. Blessed are you who have not made me a woman."[86] This statement was part of the Jewish marriage ceremony where man recited it while the bride acknowledged it by saying, "Blessed who created me according to His will."

There is an epistemological discontinuity between Judaism and Christianity, and this is contrary to what is often thought. This enforced, made-up connection between the Old and New Testaments has created an impression that the first is a backdrop to the second or a complement of it. While this connection is not of interest right now in this book, I must stress the fact that there is nothing in the New Testament to suggest any discrimination against women except a few verses mentioned in some of St. Paul's letters. Here 40% of his assistants during his missionary journeys were women who were mentioned by name and acknowledged passionately for their great help in spreading the Word. (In order to understand St. Paul's letters, it is indispensable to appreciate his historical and cultural background, but that is not the focal point of our discussion here.) However, since the adulterous woman has been exempt from punishment in Christianity and her problem was left to God to handle (the mirror of first authority), this "action" has assumed a great significance about the "concept" of women and their role in Christianity. On the other hand, the honored woman was embodied in the persona of Mary, the Virgin Mother, who is impeccably depicted far beyond any defects of a crowd of adulterous women in the Old Testament.

Infanticide continues to thrive in the mind of Arab women under many guises. She is buried alive by gender discrimination. This means that she must resist in order to survive, and this resistance may impose certain behavioral patterns on her such as avoidance, distress, and perhaps certain types of obsessions.

Today, in some underdeveloped rural areas of India, infanticide is shown in its classic form. The female fetus is killed in the womb or shortly after birth, either by strangulation, starvation, or dumping, where she is not thrown into a pit, draped and perfumed as the Arab tribes did before Islam, but in the garbage containers or sewage system.

As for China, infanticide is still carried out with governmental blessing because of the alarming increase in population; the One-child Policy is an official program, initiated in the early 1980s in which only one child per family is encouraged, and is enforced at the provincial level. There are a few exceptions, however, like if the first child is a girl or is disabled the family is allowed to have a second child. The preference for males over females has produced negative consequences, such as increased forced abortions and female infanticide, and thus the number of males has far exceeded the number of females. The killing of female fetuses is done as soon as the sex is discovered through ultrasound radiography, which is a secret, swift, and "trendy" tool that facilitates the process of modern infanticide.

Infanticide primarily has to do with female discrimination, and while it is true that this type of incident may not be "in vogue" today, it still threatens her survival, even if only internally.

⁕

There is another type of fear that is more established and pervasive in society, which is *the fear of being free*. This type of fear is publicly motivated, sometimes by oppression and pain ("I am not free!"), and sometimes by a fake commitment to morality and social and religious values ("I do not have to be free."). The female mind wages a tug of war between these two poles. It is interesting that her understanding of freedom lies entirely in its simplest sense: freedom of mere movement without any awareness of the true spirit of the word.

Today, the freedom that the Arab individual is looking for is the elimination of social, religious, political, and intellectual restrictions, whatever the cost. At the center of this claim is our belief that we are not on board the modern, global train, but, because of these restrictions, left behind. A further belief is that, because of our heritage, jumping onto this global train is something that we are unable to do. This conviction does not reflect the attitude of all Arabs, just the portion that sees the absence of freedom as primarily caused by an enforced deportation from the global train. Conversely, the other segment of the Arab population insists on covering their eyes so as not to see that Arabs are suffocating to death from a lack of freedom and not because of anything else. We build our understanding of freedom on that which we "want." As Socrates said, "Will is what the mind portrays as good," which means that our will tends to see something as good because mind decides it's so. Accordingly, don't we have to reconsider "freedom" on the basis of this statement? Or are we satisfied with the struggle for freedom within the mental frame that I mentioned previously?

As for Aristotle, he connected freedom to knowledge and this link may lead to more levels of accuracy and understanding of the concept of freedom. Freedom without knowledge tends to lead to destruction and ruin. Thus, understanding what one is asking for, and the degree of goodness in it, is a prerequisite to any claim or demand of freedom.

When we ask for freedom of expression and speech,

in return we must be aware of what we ourselves say. We should also be aware of the consequence of such a request; if it's good or has a public interest and does not seek to ruin a sector of our lives, then it may be incorporated so as to support human survival. On the other hand, if the theme of freedom is not located within our sphere of understanding and knowledge, then it will act like a wounding sword with dire consequences. Therefore, it is very absurd to believe that freedom of expression claimed by everyone from "the Atlantic to the Gulf"[87] is without any edges or limits and, most importantly, without any ensuing responsibility.

Freedom of expression and speech that leads to internal strife, for example, or an individual who unbridles himself without any attention to the results, is considered to be a clumsy freedom that only serves to relieve the person, and this is the nastiest, lowest, and narrowest level of freedom. In Western countries there is a socio-political system based on the protection of these laws, and on the legacy of democracy, that allows freedom of expression to be part of community history.

The Arab tends to use somebody else's experience of freedom and apply it without further thinking, which not only concedes that belief and viewpoint, but forces it to fit into his own social order, reflecting an inability to build a free and civilized structure based on personal experience. This also indicates that we are still at a stage where we see others as either a friend or an enemy. Much like Western values, every Arabic man is geared toward the authority of the state, the culture, and the laws.

⁃⁃⁃⁃⁃

If woman is afraid to be free, then she is afraid of something with which she is not really familiar. Throughout her long history, she's not been in a position to "know," nor was she allowed to step into any field of knowledge as a natural right. She learned from our Arab history that knowledge belongs to men and that it is one of society's taboos, as illustrated by the Tree of Knowledge and good and evil in the sacred text. Therefore, she was excluded from the realm of knowledge and authority generation after generation until she was unable to travel along the responsible road of freedom. She has been epistemologically circumcised, for knowledge not only requires freedom, forbidden to women, but also that woman take initiative at all levels (i.e., be responsible) and manage life properly. In other words, she must be equal with men in decision-making. This does not negate the integration with man; on the contrary, it negates the principle of stewardship as presented to us by sacred verses.

Fear of freedom is a fear of the ignorant person who does not know in which direction they should proceed, or what the results of their forward movement might be.

Knowledge dissolves the fear of freedom—the knowledge of who we are, what we request from ourselves, and what kind of future we are looking toward. The fear of freedom may be the only one that can be monitored in the structure of a woman's mind every time we give her the right to know: knowing her history and knowing what her duties and rights are. Freedom starts and ends with knowledge. Thus, we need to be aware of:

1. The Arab and Islamic culture is continuously reproducing itself, and always motivated by the preservation of the sacred text.

2. This cultural reproduction occurs without linking the text to any temporal or spatial happening, which means staying in the same place and building on the same old cultural foundations.

3. The word "freedom" or "free" is not featured as it is spoken in the Quran, and therefore we are not able to develop a special meaning for freedom that can belong to us and to our Arabic culture.

The only approach to the meaning of the word "freedom," as stated in the Quran, comes under the same umbrella as the abolition of slavery. This connotation is mentioned five times in the fourth and fifth Surah as well as Surah 58. It is also mentioned in (Baqarah 2:178) "O

People who Believe! Retribution is made obligatory for you in the matter of those killed unjustly; a freeman for a freeman, and a slave for a slave, and a female for a female; and for him who is partly forgiven by his brother, seek compensation with courtesy and make payment in proper manner; this is a relief and a mercy upon you, from your Lord; so after this, a painful punishment is for whoever exceeds the limits. 179, and there is life for you in retribution, O men of understanding, so that you may avoid."

Otherwise, we do not find the word in the Quran. As for Hadith, we find only one meaning of the word that contains the concept of emancipation of slavery or servitude. Other than that, we find the opposite meaning of the word as contained in Sahih Muslim, Hadith N 1847[88] and N 6922[89]. Even Umar Ibn Al Khattab,[90] in his speech about freedom, keeps the same context, which conveys the equality among people and not enslaving them. His most famous statement is, "When did you start turning people into slaves when their mothers gave birth to them as free human beings?"

This "epistemological insufficiency" of the meaning of freedom in the Arab memory is not the only one. Although the concept of freedom fits inherently with the spiritual structure of man, this concept did not assume all its other features and dimensions.

The Arab nation has built its cultural edifices on political upheavals. It was not improbable to separate the two concepts of justice and freedom in Islam, for justice is known as the correlation between God and the obedience of the human ruler, while freedom means exactly the opposite. Thus, the mind has built itself on these two poles while freedom looms as if it is a mere departure from what is already established and authorized and, of course, closer to atheism.

⸎

"I must not be free" is a statement adopted by someone who has made the choice to stick to the jurisprudence of the period and to its political and cultural necessities, and not deviate from the group. In this sense, freedom does not encompass any obedience to God, and it is an evil that is not an innate part of the human spiritual structure. Thus it should be avoided.

In fact, "Arabic freedom" is a product cultured in soil that is not prepared to blossom real fruit. Freedom is the bogeyman of Arabism because it is the reason behind civil laws, human rights, and democracy. It is a scourge allows kings and princes to abdicate their ceremonial thrones, and woman to express herself and escape the agenda of the tribe. Freedom is an open door to all imagined evils in this world against which the Arab individual does not know how to fight other than by simply upholding yet another principle.

Today, the free woman is seen as an offbeat bird and described with unkind words that do not reflect her authenticity. The mere act of self-expression may label her in a special (read: negative) category and make everyone look at her suspiciously and unintelligibly. As a free woman, she blasphemes the best image of her as portrayed by religion and society, and, it is implied, she is a violator of laws, a defector, and indifferent.

Fear of freedom based on lack of knowledge is the fear that woman persistently fights in defiance of the structure of her mind. It is a "struggle" that, if done successfully, may open the door for her to change her mental structure, and rebuild it upon a new foundation.

There is another type of fear that the Arabic female mind is familiar with, which is the so-called *fear of happiness*. This may seem like a strange fear to have, but this ability and need to rein in her desire for happiness as well as the courage to declare the subject of her joy is, indeed, real. She is a woman who both avoids pleasure and fails to achieve it; she even rejects it when offered to her, especially when it is not one of her community-authorized pleasures. Throughout history, she has found joy in very limited kinds of pleasures, so embarking upon any other kind would make her feel confused and even willing to run away from it. The word "pleasure" here does refer only to the sexual, but the spiritual, intellectual, and social, too.

In her book *Dreams of Trespass: Tales of a Harem Girlhood*, Arabic feminist and thinker Fatima Mernissi thoroughly examines her personal experience growing up in a harem in Fez, Morocco. She explains these invisible regulations that woman pays attention to when she walks into a place for the first time, rules that she is forced to consider even though they do not take her rights into account. The author notes, "The favorite activities fall, unfortunately, within the frame of the forbidden pleasures such as traveling, discovering the world, singing, dancing, and expression of opinion. Woman's happiness violates the rule. In fact, rule often seem more solid than the walls and barriers..."[91] Every woman in Mernissi's book deals with boundaries and happiness:

> 'Asmahan wanted to go to chic restaurants, dance like the French, and hold her Prince in her arms,' she would say. She wanted to waltz away with him all night, instead of standing on the sidelines behind curtains, watching him deliberate in endless, exclusively male tribal counsels. She hated the whole clan and its senseless, cruel law. All she wanted was to drift away into bubble-like moments of happiness and sensual bliss. The lady was no criminal; she

meant no harm.[92]

The relationship between woman and her own inner channels, which provides her with various pleasures, is an uneasy one. These channels are subject to major censorship, led by society and the darkest part of her mind, and are distorted and unusable due to laws of social customs and fanatic religious systems that have accumulated within her. They are similar to clots that clog the artery walls, preventing the flow of blood to the heart and often killing the person. Arabic woman is dead in this sense because she carries out orders without any positive spiritual and emotional interaction. Even today, the majority of Arab women avoid conflicting with those orders and so become convinced of their slow and ceremonial death in this "counterfeit paradise" of the modern Arab world.

What helps to unblock and lubricate these channels is something unthinkable: her financial independence. Allowing woman to have some financial autonomy would permit her to run her own show, and having some measure of control over herself would open the floodgates for her to enter the Harem of sealed desires and taste the thrill of discovery with silent happiness.

Her economic independence would put her at a distance from any kind of dependency on other people's pleasure, so she would not only share her husband's joy or allow herself to enjoy family and social activities, but also would be able to initiate her own pleasure based on what she and she alone likes.

During my travels, I have discovered many "small pleasures" that were not available to me in the early period of my life in Syria, such as sitting in a cozy corner in a coffee shop or public library and writing, seated on the grass in a public park and reading, walking along the beach alone for hours, having a quiet lunch in a small restaurant, and chatting with a male friend without fear of what people might say about my behavior or that they would invent ridiculous stories about "us." All these pleasures that were elusive to me in the past are now available as a result of the change in the political decisions in Syria and the awesome security that allows women to go out at night without being intercepted, while other Arab states still lag far behind in the belief that women need to be empowered.[93] I say this with the deep conviction that there are still lots of laws and regulations concerning women that need to be changed in Syria, knowing that the road to enlightenment is still very long and difficult to travel for those who are willing to write these rules and regulations off.

◦◦◦◦◦

There are pleasures that are considered even more dangerous than those mentioned above; those are related to "knowledge." The inability to visualize other pleasures or "invent" something more important for oneself is entirely dependent on the fact that knowledge was not available to woman, because there is an inherently strong relation between knowledge and pleasure.

In Imam Abu Hamid Muhammad al-Ghazali's[94] beautiful book *The Chemistry of Happiness*, he states:

> Anyone who will look into the matter will see that happiness is necessarily linked with the knowledge of God. Each faculty of ours delights in that for which it was created: lust delights in accomplishing desire, anger in taking vengeance, the eye in seeing beautiful objects, and the ear in hearing harmonious sounds. The highest function of the soul of man is the perception of truth; in this accordingly it finds its special delight. Even in trifling matters, such, as learning chess, this holds good, and the higher the subject-matter of the knowledge obtained the greater the delight. A man would be pleased at being admitted into the confidence of a prime minister, but how much more if the king makes an intimate of him and discloses state secrets to him!

In fact, Imam al-Ghazali does not limit pleasure to knowing God alone, but uses it as a platform to know everything related to "Him." It is the pleasure of a more comprehensive knowledge that cannot be nullified by death. Unlike physical desires, this pleasure is an everlasting one, revealing and eternal in a certain sense. It is the pleasure of the "knower" or the "mediator" of the world who is seeking his own essence and the reason behind his existence in the first place.

It is a pleasure "committed" by those who have become bored enough by low-ranking desires that they are no longer eager to struggle for them. Therefore, the types of pleasure that woman is looking for are primitive and lower in grade, although elevating them correlates significantly to the degree of her knowledge and awareness.

In fact, the female mind, which I believe is still at the mirror's stage as I mentioned in chapter two, needs more time and maturity to be able to give up the lower-grade pleasures and penetrate into deeper and higher layers of real pleasures. The pleasure sought by her now is the pleasure of "knowing her own mind" and fulfilling its first desires. Her mind seeks instantaneous pleasure, such as driving a car, living independently in an apartment of her own, getting academic certificates that give her the right to work and occupy a higher position, choosing the spouse that she thinks is right for her, selecting a dress that fits her taste and only her taste, being able to go out whenever she likes, enjoying freedom of expression, and, of course, having the right to financial independence and self-determinism. These are all "pleasures" that embody the minimum bill of human rights, and yet they have nothing to do with higher grades of real pleasure, which is knowledge.

Subsequently, it is not fear of pleasure or happiness that she feels, but rather the ignorance of and inability to invent them, for happiness is completely an inner creative act, not an "event" or something that "happens" to a person. On the contrary, it is an internal vigilance crowned with understanding (i.e. knowledge) and topped with ultimate conviction.

❧

There is another type of fear that the female mind experiences, which is *the fear of responsibility*. Islam is known for the close and direct relationship between God and human being, and no Muslim is hindered from praying to and communicating with God anytime and anywhere: "And O dear Prophet (Mohammed - peace and blessings be upon him), when My bondmen question you concerning Me, then surely I am close; I answer the prayer of the supplicant when he calls on Me, so they must obey Me and believe in Me, so that they may attain guidance." (Baqarah 2:186)

However, fear of responsibility is due to something that happens all the time, which is man's self-inauguration as mediator between the world and woman. If her relationship with God does not need any mediator, how then does man consider himself the mediator between her and the world? Isn't this interference the hidden reason that implants a tendency within her to avoid responsibility, which has become inherent in her mind throughout the ages and has killed in her any sense of initiative or leadership?

The same concept is encountered in Christianity, especially in Saint Paul's messages: "But I want you to understand that the head of every man is Christ, the head of a woman is her husband, and the head of Christ is God. For a man ought not to cover his head, since he is the image and glory of God; but woman is the glory of man." (Corinthian 11:3) And: "For man was not made from woman, but woman from man." (Corinthian 11:8) And: "Neither was man created for woman, but woman for man." (Corinthian 11:9)

The revelation here connects spiritual paternity to leadership, i.e. a firm grasp of initiative and self-determined responsibility. This "divine" link between leadership and responsibility is understood by anyone who is a believer, whatever his religion may be. The responsibility is vested in the religious guide who is always a male.

When the female mind receives this divine concept of responsibility, she has to show complete obedience like a little kid listening to the guidance of her parents. It is a child's mind within the sacred text, and this mind must not grow up because the text itself is also not able to grow up, i.e. not able to change or be changed. The sequence of responsibility, in apostolic Christianity and Islam, has always been from God to man to woman. Even the Virgin Mary, who is considered the Mother of God, has not received any apostolic responsibility, but only given the title of Holy Mother.

The examples of priesthood presented by the Bible have included only men. This includes the first priesthood of the Patriarchs (such as Noah, Job, Abraham, Isaac, and Jacob), of the Aaronic or Melchizedek priesthood, or the priesthood of the Apostles and their successors of bishops. Any priesthood of women is a mere invention or fabrication in religion; thus, her responsibilities have been limited to include only the social activities such as educating children, iconography, sewing the priests' garments, and taking care of orphans and people in need, etc. There is no evidence in the Bible or history of women teaching men or holding any position in the priesthood hierarchy.

The Imamate of Islam, which is the highest level of religious responsibility, has a similar chain of command. Muslim Imams are considered the commanders-in-chief and successors of the Prophet, despite the fact that Islamic nations have agreed that revelation and legislation stopped after the death of the Prophet.

There are many descriptions of the functions and qualifications of the Imam. Initially, Imamate was a responsibility or a social authorization by which the nation granted an Imam the right to run and manage its matters. However, this does not mean that an Imam has inherited full power from the Prophet or Apostle, as is the case in all political-religious positions with few exceptions. Imamate is an activation of the judiciary, executive, and legislative powers. Moreover, the theory of social authorization is one of two theories about the "terms and conditions of Imam," and as such does not assume that he should be the most knowledgeable among the nation nor the most aware of the established laws and politics—unless he has the same otherworldliness abilities that were acquired by the prophet Mohammed.

However, there is another theory that believes the Imamate is a divine mandate. The followers of this theory admit that prophecy, the message, and the revelation stopped after the death of the Prophet. Nevertheless, they still believe that the Imam "is the most knowledgeable among the nation, and the most skillful in judiciary and the origins of the religion and its branches as well as the most reliable to defend the Harem of Islam, and its set of beliefs and knowledge with all the other qualifications that Prophet Mohammed had."[95]

Since the responsibilities of the Prophet were huge, his successor had to be at least "intact from slippage and infallible,"[96] which has not been the case when it comes to understanding women in any era of the Arabs' "blessed" times.

Thus, the responsibility became, at its highest level, synonymous with masculinity, and accordingly it has been implanted in the Arab female mind that even the most minor and lowest-grade responsibilities are simply another word for manhood.

Free education in some Arab countries has revolutionized woman. She not only became interested in learning, but it also enabled her to truly reach the highest levels of knowledgeable and cognitive pleasure, and to request the highest degree of responsibility for herself: Imamate, priestly authority, and leadership. In fact, I've heard that some women claim to reach the highest level of priesthood not because of their eagerness to ascend to that position, but because they want to defy gender discrimination even in prayer.

Woman is now not only the birth-giver and breast-feeder, but she also wears the garments of Imamate, legislator, and law drafter. Now she is right there at the top echelon of responsibility: direct mediator between herself and God. Nevertheless, the importance of this matter does not come from her desire to break the taboo of Sunnah, but from her strong aspiration to equality as a free soul able and willing to give.

The fear of responsibility in the Arab female mind is on the verge of collapse. It is true that she has been trained to walk behind her man a least a meter, but that distance is getting shorter in her mind and her stride, little by little. However, we live in a time of unprecedented confrontations where too many people have mastered the art of quick persuasion and the ability to establish confidence in others, and now they are ready to "sell" it with a sleight of hand or through their verbal dexterity.

While I ask woman to abandon her fears, I encourage her at the same time to adopt a healthy fear that can protect her against all unsolicited approaches, although I certainly know the difficulty of doing that. The Western culture that encourages woman to show courtesy and kindness in her dialogue with strange men offers her in return the potential expectations that put her in danger. On the contrary, the Arab woman, in spite of her permanent precaution of man, is victimized by him sexually, spiritually, economically, and socially. In truth, neither civility and openness nor reticence can protect woman against this risk.

Certainly, there is a healthy and natural kind of fear that is instilled in human beings for their safety and survival: it is the fear of the unknown and the forces that are beyond their perception.

Sex: The Duality of Sanctification and Delinquency

"I am nowhere if not in the bodies of all women."
—Buddha[97]

Sex was not a subject matter that was talked about in our house. Even my dad's high level of education did not allow the discussion of this topic to be part of our daily life, but instead kept it shamefully under wraps. My parents avoided jokes, hints, or any other scenario that had sexual connotations in front of us. Even the American or French television shows had to be turned off right away if a kiss were about to happen, and most of the time my brothers and I were required to leave the living room or distract ourselves so we wouldn't see what was happening on the TV screen.

My first introduction to the subject of sex came

from a nun while at summer camp in one of the Lebanese mountain resorts where we, Christian youth, used to receive additional education in religion and life by both religious and laic mentors. In 1974 on a beautiful moonlit night in a small town called Harissa,[98] where the famous statue of the majestic Virgin Mary oversees the shores of Beirut from above, we were sitting in a circle around our spiritual mentor, a nun, listening to the first talk about sex. A religious song "We Are Awake the Night", composed by Ziad Rahbani,[99] was playing quietly near us. Everything was just divine and perfect in that starry night. I was not yet thirteen years old, and my body was relatively small, but I had an attentive soul and a confused awareness. I had to summon enormous strength in order to understand what this introduction that we were listening to was about. Apparently, it was about the relationship between women and men.

The nun's indirect approach and carefulness made me unable to understand what she meant at first. She talked neither about love nor spiritual bond nor the real integration between femininity and masculinity. Instead, she talked only about the process of sexual intercourse and how it happens because, as she said, "I prefer that you know it from us, your spiritual mentors, and what exactly it is, instead of learning a distorted version of it from other resources."

She talked about the sperm and the egg, and said that the meeting between these two is called insemination, during which the woman becomes pregnant. When a friend, sitting close to me, asked her how, practically speaking, this happens, the nun replied, "Of course, man and woman must lay next to each other first...." Ironically, the rest of the statement was left to our crippled, infantile imaginations to figure out.

While I used to interpret the word sex to mean love no matter what the context, I realized later that this incredible amount of knowledge about the relationship between woman and man all boiled down to one thing in our Arab culture: lust, or pleasure. It also meant men's rights and his actual stewardship. Thus, the concept of sex is very confusing to the Arabic female mind and is jumbled with a lot of assumptions, perceptions, and false and painful truths. With time, I have seen that these perceptions about sex are, to a large degree, the same to Muslim and Christian women in Syria, save for some liberal, rich families where freedom was a historical legacy. These perceptions began when Syria was under French command, flourishing from the occupation to the present day.[100]

Today, the Syrian woman, whether Muslim or Christian, is considered among all Arab women to be the most liberal and unchained intellectually, in spite of all the challenges and discriminatory laws that are imposed upon her. This is due, perhaps, to the nature of the Syrian political system, which strongly believes in the empowerment of woman, as mentioned in the Constitution of the Syrian Arab Republic.

The separation of religion and state in Syria, and non-allowance of the intervention of religious authorities to take over in the political and social arenas no matter what, has given the attribute of secularism to Syrian society. In doing so, religion itself is protected against all kinds of practices and acts that may degrade its spirituality or turn Syrian society into a one-size-fits-all community.

However, sex, both theoretically and practically, remains one of the most oppressive taboos for woman. Sex is the unseen backdrop of her fears that has paralyzed the structure of her mind. In fact, cognitive dimension was almost absent in the upbringing of Arab women as a general rule, and consequently, sex has taken its shape and dimensions from what was available to her in the knowledge and culture markets in the environment.

The sacred text tells us that the sexual act was "committed" only after Adam and Eve had discovered their nudity, as though the sexual act needed a preparatory event to pave the way for it to be shown as an exceptional revelation to them, and this revelation was not exposed to man alone, but to both of them. However, our inherited sexual culture has taken the responsibility, in both the religious and folkloric arenas, of training woman in this physical "labor," rather than transcending the sexual act to make it a spiritual and sacred one, in the true sense of the word. On the contrary, it has been portrayed carefully and accurately while forgetting that in the midst of worshipping the functions of the male body, and his priorities and rights, which the female was also permitted to "know," in the Biblical sense.

Just as political leadership, Imamate, and stewardship are reserved to man, sex, too, has been taken over by him; it is man who has established the rules and regulations that have become instilled in the structure of woman's mind and has made up part of her idea about what sex and her role in it is. Man was the sole "knower" in many stages throughout history, thus he is the "owner" of the decision socially and functionally, and he is the one who can make hypotheses and conclusions, leaving little space for woman to maneuver within. What little space is left is reserved for Cinderella and Scheherazade—in other words, the subjugated woman. This is not man's fault, and is neither a physiological aberration nor a mental dysfunction, and he does not have an inherent inclination to purposefully harm woman. History tells us that many women were freed and empowered with the help of men, and that man would not extend his "playground" without the permission of the collective Arabic regressive mind.

This knowledge, as we have seen, is not one of the features of the Arab female upbringing, but has remained a "gift," owned by few women throughout history until recently when education has opened the door for her to question her role in sex and sexuality, her nature as a woman, and her functional integration with man. The defects in the religious and social ways the Arabic woman has been raised have been revealed by her education, so from now on woman must start her long battle against the vicious system from scratch and on the basis of a new and real understanding of her condition.

The legendary fall of Adam and Eve from paradise has automatically linked sex to religion, or knowledge. This sudden human attention to the nakedness of the body was grounds for new moral legislation of Halal and Haram (i.e. "permissible and forbidden"), and thus nudity—the result of seeking knowledge—was categorized as taboo. Knowledge was originally considered sinful because it incites awareness, opens the eyes, and draws a roadmap towards cognition and decision making, and all these things are usually assigned to the most sacred authorities of the highest rank. Thus, knowledge is sacred, semi-divine, and sinful if "stolen" from God by a slave or mere mortal. This is what we have been taught by Adam and Eve's story of nudity.

Whoever "owns" knowledge owns the key to decision-making and law-drafting and freedom of action. As a result, most dictatorial regimes in the world tend to deliberately block the resources of knowledge in an effort to prevent people from realizing the bad condition of their lives and revolting.

Woman was forced to follow the same footpath throughout history. She was isolated and detached from almost all resources of knowledge in order to keep her within the small patios allocated to her, those built away from the main door of the house where the key is always in the pocket of her breadwinner.

When the Universal Declaration of Human Rights was announced, regarded by many on this planet as an alternative international secular "religion," woman did not fully take advantage of it because the Declaration terms neglected her physiological specificity, femininity, and need for integration with man. Moreover, this Declaration did not have a positive impact on all communities because some considered it an attempted "coup" not only against society, but against the sacred text itself. And the reason for that is because this Declaration ignored the cultural relativism of each society, and tried to categorize all communities on this planet under one banner of general principles, which were always according to the authorities of these communities.

Remarkably, the ancient religions considered prostitution, the offering of the naked body as a sexual oblation, as something sacred, spiritual, and worthy of ovation. For prostitutes in ancient temples who offered their bodies as a sacrifice to priests or for the amusement of pilgrims, sex was not connected with prohibition in their minds. To them, sex was an act that was part of the cognitive, social, and cultural atmosphere of that civilization. A prostitute's body that was offered as a sacrifice to God in the temple was a body that allowed its "owner" to somehow atone for the initial sinful sexual act, but this time in front of the eyes of authority (knowledge) and with its approval.

This sex act is sacred because it is approved and blessed by authority, and thus has risen above its sin to enter the sphere of sanctification and acceptance. Later on, this practice evolved so that the prostitute left the temple and entered the most noble of palaces as a mistress on whom lots of effort and money was spent for education and other training. Once again, the connection between sex and knowledge was revealed (sex being one of magnificent gates to knowledge), and sex was no longer penitential for the sake of God. Instead, it was now linked to spiritual and intellectual pleasure, so the prostitute was not merely learning the art of how to arouse or distract the pilgrims, but also skills such as the martial arts, rhetoric, fashion, cooking, landscaping, poetry, flower arrangement, languages, and much more. Obviously, I did not use the prostitute as an ideal example of woman, but rather because I wanted to draw attention to this permanent connection between knowledge and the more controversial sex, prostitution, and nudity, which are the opposite of obscuration, decency, and virginity (ignorance).

This concept of sex, in its most spiritual sense, stripped of its cloak of bawdy excitement, reveals a better understanding of the role and position of woman. In Buddhism, conversely, sex began with the canonization and worshipping of woman and was regarded as the embodiment of Buddha, or complete wisdom, only to be considered later as a more suspicious and conservative subject by religious and cultural society.

It is remarkable that prostitution is condemned because that means woman is selling her body to every Tom, Dick or Harry, which violates the sanctity and sacredness of this body. Spiritual prostitution (the prostitution of politics, culture, and thought) is not condemned the same way because it is the type of prostitution in which all its standards and norms are subject to interpretation, while physical prostitution is simply more evident and definitive, and its language and appearance are more transparent or, literally, naked.

However, before I get to the concept of contemporary sex in the Arab woman's mental structure, let me go through the cultures that preceded the Arab one, which have left their mark here and there due to the inevitable process of acculturation.

⤳⤳⟨⟩⤵⤶

The first characteristic of Buddhism is that it follows "the middle way," which is a Buddhist term that implies a balanced approach to life and the guideline for one's impulses and behavior. The teachings of Buddha were recorded by his students and then codified over the next 500 years, and this selection that follows is one of the most beautiful teachings about "the middle way" in which we can find the illusion of salvation through the two extremes of behavior: austerity or indulgence in pleasures.

> There are two extremes, O bhikkhus, which the man who has given up the world ought not to follow—the habitual practice, on the one hand, of self-indulgence which is unworthy, vain and fit only for the worldly-minded and the habitual practice, on the other hand, of self-mortification, which is painful, useless and unprofitable. Neither abstinence from fish or flesh, nor going naked, nor shaving the head, nor wearing matted hair, nor dressing in a

119

rough garment, nor covering oneself with dirt, nor sacrificing to Agni, will cleanse a man who is not free from delusions. Reading the Vedas, making offerings to priests, or sacrifices to the gods, self-mortification by heat or cold, and many such penances performed for the sake of immortality, these do not cleanse the man who is not free from delusions. Anger, drunkenness, obstinacy, bigotry, deception, envy, self-praise, disparaging others, superciliousness and evil intentions constitute uncleanness; not verily the eating of flesh. A middle path, O bhikkhus, avoiding the two extremes, has been discovered by the Tathagata—a path which opens the eyes, and bestows understanding, which leads to peace of mind, to the higher wisdom, to full enlightenment, to Nirvana! What is that middle path, O bhikkhus, avoiding these two extremes, discovered by the Tathagata—that path which opens the eyes, and bestows understanding, which leads to peace of mind, to the higher wisdom, to full enlightenment, to Nirvana? Let me teach you, O bhikkhus, the middle path, which keeps aloof from both extremes. By suffering, the emaciated devotee produces confusion and sickly thoughts in his mind. Mortification is not conducive even to worldly knowledge; how much less to a triumph over the senses![101]

As for Tantra, it is remarkable how its spiritual disciplines insist on evolving into higher states of awareness by guiding or rejecting the senses and any degraded states of awareness. Tantra demonstrates how complete spiritual liberation cannot be done if one is restricting a part of one's being. It is a very insightful method of energetic meditation that increases awareness by using the senses to take a human being far beyond the territory of the senses. In this context, sacred sexuality is a spiritual path and is practiced with an air of sacredness.

The philosophy of Tantra is an authentic way of living, connecting the body, mind, and spirit within a live and homogeneous system. Tantrism uses the physical reality as a means to reveal the spiritual aspect of it, because according to this text everything in the universe is complete as it is and borders exist only within the scope of the mind. In fact, thought has no limits, and the individual's tantric experiences are incomplete as long as there are limits inside of him. Tantra believes and teaches that woman is the original energy from whom everything emerges, as well as the "guardian" of this energy. Further, according to the tantric texts, this limitless energy exists in both woman and man and when awoken, the spiritual sexual power can be channeled creatively.

Tantric sexual intercourse between man and woman is regarded as a pure activation of this innovative and deep creative energy, for the aim of human life is union with Supreme awareness and integration with the Divine. During intercourse, man and woman, at the peak moment, experience a kind of emptiness of the mind and freeness of ideation. At this moment, all thoughts vanish, and this mental vacuum is the conduit for the "descending" of Divine joy. It is a moment of temporary death and the flow of joy within oneself. It is a moment where self-identity disappears, turning into a pure, vibrant energy that is free of central selfishness.

Amazingly, this tantric description of the sacred concept of intercourse is probably the deepest and most accurate that I've read about sex. This profound spiritual joy has nothing whatsoever to do with sex as I have known it as an Arabic woman.

The moment barriers vanish, the moment of freedom, is totally bizarre to the Arab woman, for every time we meet such a moment we do not know what it is simply because we've never experienced it before. It is a sacred moment without identity or limits. This deep moment scares us, once we are aware of it, because it tends to unveil our identity's Hijab, and we have been taught to "wrap" ourselves up with our unmistakable identities while sacredness lies elsewhere. In other words, it is a moment of awareness and understanding (knowledge), and therefore it is forbidden and sinful.

While we know that the sexual peak will continue "for a moment," the philosophy of tantric Buddhism teaches us that it lasts for hours, if only we knew how. Making love becomes an activity with spiritual results that last much longer and with deeper effect than just the momentary physical climax. It is not a need like food and water, but it has an entirely other dimension: it is a way to communicate and unite with the Supreme reality and a desire to contact the original source of life (knowledge and knowledge's holder). Thus, tantric sex is a universally contemplative experience. It is love, prayer, and relaxation in the heart completely, while physical sex captures only one dimension of the meaning of sex.

While sex is regarded as a sinful act and must be controlled in the Middle East in general, it is not the case in Buddhist tantric thought; however, it may become impure if it involves the sin of selfishness and utter delusion. Sex is venereal to most of us, especially to the Arabic woman who considers it a duty to her man, and meditation to the Buddhist because it embodies freedom of self.

It is interesting to note that Buddha did not become a teacher until he discovered this energy within himself, while the idea behind this Quranic verse "If you fear that you will not deal justly with the orphan girls, then marry those that please you of [other] women, two or three or four. But if you fear that you will not be just, then [marry only] one or those your right hand possesses. That is more suitable that you may not incline [to injustice]" (Surat An-Nisā)" reflects very clearly the issue of justice for woman.

In fact, we are asking the Arabic woman here to be able to play, for the first time, an instrument that she has never touched; we are asking her to give an excellent performance without "knowingness."

❧

Swami Vivekananda,[102] a young Hindu monk, talked about the ability of this energy in one of his texts called "Sexual Power":

> We are thinking of the soul as body, but we must separate it from sense and thought. Then alone can we know we are immortal. Change implies the duality of cause and effect, and all that changes must be mortal. This proves that the body cannot be immortal, nor can the mind, because both are constantly changing. Only the unchangeable can be immortal, because there is nothing to act upon it. We do not become it, we are it; but we have to clear away the veil of ignorance that hides the truth from us. The body is objectified thought. The nerve

center at the base of the spine near the sacrum is most important. It is the seat of the generative substance of the sexual energy and is symbolized by the Yogi as a triangle containing a tiny serpent coiled up in it. This sleeping serpent is called Kundalini, and to raise this Kundalini is the whole object of Raja-Yoga [Royal Science of Union]. The great sexual force, raised from animal action and sent upward to the great dynamo of the human system, the brain, and there stored up, becomes Ojas or spiritual force. All good thought, all prayer, resolves a part of that animal energy into Ojas and helps to give us spiritual power. This Ojas is the real man and in human beings alone is it possible for this storage of Ojas to be accomplished. One in whom the whole animal sex force has been transformed into Ojas is a god. He speaks with power, and his words regenerate the world. The Yogi pictures this serpent as being slowly lifted from stage to stage until the highest, the pineal gland, is reached. No man or woman can be really spiritual until the sexual energy, the highest power possessed by man, has been converted into Ojas. No force can be created; it can only be directed. Therefore we must learn to control the grand powers that are already in our hands and by will power make them spiritual instead of merely animal. Thus it is clearly seen that chastity is the corner-stone of all morality and of all religion. The same laws apply to the married and the single. If one wastes the most potent forces of one's being, one cannot become spiritual."[103]

Vivekananda's words make me ponder this huge difference in approaching the subject of sex between Buddhists and the rest of us, though we all live on same planet. The Buddhist thought, like ours, understands the value of chastity, but surpasses the form to the essence right away by considering chastity a channel that leads towards a more spiritual sphere.

As an Arab Christian woman, nobody taught me the deeper dimensions of any human experience, especially on the subject of sex. I did not learn that sex has a cognitive value from my education, and my parents and mentors did not touch on this subject much, if ever. Chastity is essential in Christianity to the extent that it overshadows any other consideration with regard to the subject of sex, and in fact the regulation of sexual activity in the fourth century AD was one of the main concerns of all Christian churches at the time. This was a way to ensure that ecclesiastical law was the only reference code with which church leaders controlled the intimate lives of Christians.

Anyone not acquainted with The Canons of the

Holy Fathers Assembled at The Council of Gangra in 340 AD may be shocked to know that sixty-four out of eighty-one canon laws are related to the regulation of sexual relations amongst Christians.[104] Moreover, between the third and tenth centuries, the ecclesiastical references issued ordinances that prohibited sex on Saturdays, Wednesdays, and Fridays, as well as during Lent before the feast of Easter, Christmas, and Pentecost, and all are due to religious reasons. Historian John Boswell discovered that the church allowed spouses to have marital intercourse only forty-four days out of 365, subtracting fasting, menstrual days, and the Saints Days.[105]

Sex in Christianity meant only one thing: chastity. Although Jesus was not too concerned with the daily life of Christians, and did not pay much attention to organizing, regulating or putting taboos on their sex lives, he was still implying it while talking on the subject of chastity and adultery. At every opportunity, Jesus asked his followers to commit to chastity for the sake of the "kingdom of heaven," as contained in Chapter XIX of the Gospel of Matthew:

> The Pharisees also came unto him, tempting him, and saying unto him, Is it lawful for a man to put away his wife for every cause? And he answered and said unto them, Have ye not read, that he which made them at the beginning made them male and

female, And said, For this cause shall a man leave father and mother, and shall cleave to his wife: and they twain shall be one flesh? Wherefore they are no more twain, but one flesh. What therefore God hath joined together, let not man put asunder. They say unto him, Why did Moses then command to give a writing of divorcement, and to put her away? He saith unto them, Moses because of the hardness of your hearts suffered you to put away your wives: but from the beginning it was not so. And I say unto you, Whosoever shall put away his wife, except it be for fornication, and shall marry another, committeth adultery: and whoso marrieth her which is put away doth commit adultery. His disciples say unto him, If the case of the man be so with his wife, it is not good to marry. But he said unto them, All men cannot receive this saying, save they to whom it is given. For there are some eunuchs, which were so born from their mother's womb: and there are some eunuchs, which were made eunuchs of men: and there be eunuchs, which have made themselves eunuchs for the kingdom of heaven's sake. He that is able to receive it, let him receive it.[106]

Jesus did not explain why neither the virtue of

chastity nor the sin of adultery was the way to the kingdom of heaven, and neither did he explain whether this path was even accessible by a commitment to chastity. On the other hand, Jesus could not condemn the adulterous woman whose blame, as he assumed, surpassed him as an authority. He said "He that is without sin among you, let him first cast a stone at her" without making forgiveness an incentive so that she would reconsider her behavior and her life. In doing so, Jesus turned the "Jewish mind" upside down.[107]

The New Testament is filled with such attitudes that implicitly request you neglect the verbatim laws of Moses and live up to the highest standards where only the symbolic meaning of the word is acknowledged and endorsed. While Jesus did not address the subject directly, preferring to speak in parables and symbols, St. Paul decided that dealing with these matters was mandatory, especially at a time when chastity needed to be redefined.

In his first letter to the Corinthians, St. Paul put the "idolaters, adulterers, and gays" on the same level as those who were deprived of the Kingdom of God. In order to leave a bigger impact as a result of his speech, he commandeered ownership of the body from the individual himself and made it one of the things that is subject to God directly as well as owned by him. "Know ye not that your body is the temple of the Holy Ghost which is in you, which ye have of God, and ye are not your own?"[108] Thus,

God is not only the owner of the knowledge, but also owner of the body of the believer, and therefore one must be removed from the vulgarity of dealing with the body. In fact, Paul, in his speech, wanted everyone to be "as I am," i.e. a virgin and full-time worshipper, even married couples and widows. "But if they cannot contain, let them marry: for it is better to marry than to burn."[109]

Chastity is not so much the problem as the solution and is located beyond right or wrong. The problem is considering sexual contact a sin, as defined by the Ecumenical Councils and in the laws that the church imposed on spousal intercourse during the first century. The church overreacted when they perceived a danger in this sexual energy because they feared it may slip out of their jurisdiction and take an uncontrollable direction.

Religion and philosophy have spent relentless time and effort in attempting to discard the sexual act and sanctify its result (reproduction). Perhaps we can find in St. Augustine's writings some of these philosophical and theological tendencies to interpret things without taking into account the understanding of human nature and sexual motivation. Such tendencies are there in St. Paul's thoughts, too, adulterated with Hellenistic traces. Although he understood the concept of resurrection and Divine revelation very well and gave them their symbolic features, he remained literal on the subject of chastity and sex as he linked them directly to faith in God. Unlike Tantra, this effort has no connotations whatsoever, nor any spiritual supremacy.

As for St. Augustine's view of woman, sex, and reproduction, it was very complicated. The most prominent of his blunders was his idea that the original sin of Adam and Eve had introduced significant chaos into human sexual desire. He believed that when Adam and Eve disobeyed God, this was done strictly within their bodies. And the consequence of this original sin, Augustine theorized, was that human beings were no longer able to monitor and control themselves.

In his treatise "On Marriage and Concupiscence," St. Augustine says:

> The union, then, of male and female for the purpose of procreation is the natural good of marriage. But he makes bad use of this good who uses it bestially, so that his intention is on the gratification of lust, instead of the desire of offspring. With respect, however, to what I ascribed to the nature of marriage, that the male and the female are united together as associates for procreation, and consequently do not defraud each other (forasmuch as every associated state has a natural abhorrence of a fraudulent companion), although even men without

faith possess this palpable blessing of nature, yet, since they use it not in faith, they only turn it to evil and sin. In like manner, therefore, the marriage of believers converts to the use of righteousness that carnal concupiscence by which 'the flesh lusteth against the Spirit.' For they entertain the firm purpose of generating offspring to be regenerated— that the children who are born of them as 'children of the world' may be born again and become 'sons of God.' Wherefore all parents who do not beget children with this intention, this will, this purpose, of transferring them from being members of the first man into being members of Christ, but boast as unbelieving parents over unbelieving children— however circumspect they be in their cohabitation, studiously limiting it to the begetting of children— really have no conjugal chastity in themselves. For inasmuch as chastity is a virtue, hating fornication as its contrary vice, and as all the virtues (even those whose operation is by means of the body) have their seat in the soul, how can the body be in any true sense said to be chaste, when the soul itself is committing fornication against the true God? Now such fornication the holy psalmist censures when he says: 'For, lo, they that are far from Thee shall perish: Thou hast destroyed all them that go a whoring from Thee.' There is, then, no true chastity, whether conjugal, or vidual, or virginal, except that which devotes itself to true faith. For though consecrated virginity is rightly preferred to marriage, yet what Christian in his sober mind would not prefer catholic Christian women who have been even more than once married, to not only vestals, but also to heretical virgins? So great is the avail of faith, of which the apostle says, 'Whatsoever is not of faith is sin;' and of which it is written in the Epistle to the Hebrews, 'Without faith it is impossible to please God.'[110]

St. Augustine insists on spiritual chastity first, otherwise all other chastity is not possible, unless granted itself to God. There is not a single Christian, he argues, who has a portentous mind and yet accepts marriage with a Catholic woman who has married more than once. So, everything is connected with its raison d'être based on how close to or far from God it is, otherwise it is invalid. He denies any other human "experience" that might emerge from sexual contact between men and women and, accordingly, he absolutely does not consider it a path leading to any spiritual threshold. Chastity here is merely an ethical and behavioral courtesy that is binding without any other sentimental feature.

According to St. Augustine, sex has only one dimension that, in order to serve the Divine will of God, cannot be avoided, and is detached from the purpose of the sexual act itself as if it were quite unable to launch a higher spiritual plane. The whole Augustine and Pauline way of thinking does not see any perspective in the sexual act; rather, they addressed it as a sinful issue that needed handling so as not to distract the person from worshipping God full-time.

It is interesting that condemning the subject of sex from the perspective of the church, not Jesus Christ, is the direct cause of the "sexual revolution" that took place in the West after World War II. According to the Bible (the first letter of St. Paul to the Corinthians), marriage and pleasing God are two different things. Marriage indicates that man is so involved in this world and so busy satisfying his partner that refraining from marriage is preferable. Thus, Christianity praises celibacy, adopts it, and considers marriage as an impediment to the salvation of man and as a real distraction from the Lord.

Like his antecedent, St. Augustine believed that sex was a threat to spiritual upgrading: "I know nothing which brings the manly mind down from the heights more than a woman's caresses and that joining of bodies without which one cannot have a wife."[111] Furthermore, he says, "Man's transgression [i.e. Adam and Eve's sin] did not annul the blessing of fertility bestowed upon him before he sinned, but infected it with the disease of lust."[112]

Like St. Paul, he again glorifies celibacy and sees sex as a shameful and disgraceful act that is "polluted" by original sin. He also ranked monasticism, which is a condition that must displayed by nuns and priests, in a higher place than marriage. As for the libido, he considered it a disease that infected man after his fall, and thus it was rather embarrassing to pay attention to the pleasure in sex.

The Christian clergy, who has adopted this viewpoint, was not immune from slipping into the trap of opposing human nature. "It was only towards the end of the thirteenth century that the celibacy of the clergy was rigidly enforced. The clergy, of course, continued to have illicit relations with women...."[113] Further, "Pope John XII was condemned for adultery and incest; the abbot-elect of St. Augustine, at Canterbury, in 1171 was found to have seventeen illegitimate children in a single village; Henry III, Bishop of Leige, was deposed in 1274 for having sixty-five illegitimate children."[114]

When the influence of the Christian Church on the Western world faded, and its control over the state became limited, the signs of revolution started to emerge in reaction to the sexual suppression. Thus, the ownership of the human body moved from God's hands to man's, who became henceforth the sole authority as far as his own needs and desires were concerned. Psychologists, counselors, and moralists have replaced bishops and the clergy, "free love" has replaced celibacy, chastity, and monasticism, and cohabitation has replaced traditional, religious marriage. Thus, in the name of democracy and freedom, family cohesion weakened and many new concepts and terminology entered into society, such as "single mother," "illegal pregnancy," the idea of kids running away from home, and the erosion of parenting values. However, the sexual revolution did not continue with the same momentum with which it started, but took a different turn, as is always the case with any cultural or ideological change, and when the defects and features surfaced, the first injury was towards woman, for her distinctive characteristics were not taken into account.

Thus, the storm of "free sex" and "sex for sex" was born in reaction to the errors of this line of extreme liberalism. Today, Western society has realized the importance of "responsible sex" within a framework of controls that takes into consideration both the spirit and the body. One example is the widespread occurrence of AIDS that wiped out over 35 million people in less than a quarter of a century. This disease is just one feature of the sexual revolution; meanwhile, both Asian and Middle Eastern Christians and Muslims adhered to their values and, for the most part, avoided this consequence.

❦

So what is the solution?

The Islamic name for marriage is "Nikah" and literally translates to "sexual intercourse." As a religion, Islam is aware that the natural needs, especially sexual ones, of humankind must be satisfied legitimately and legally, and marriage and sex are considered signs of the power of God: "And among His signs is that He created spouses for you from yourselves for you to gain rest from them, and kept love and mercy between yourselves; indeed in this are signs for the people who ponder." (Ruum 30:21) He says in another verse: "And enjoin in marriage those among you who are not married, and your deserving slaves and bondwomen; if they are poor, Allah will make them wealthy by His munificence; and Allah is Most Capable, All Knowing." (Noor 24:32)

The emphasis in Islam on the idea of marriage (Nikah) comes from an awareness of the natural needs of human beings, and adopts a strong attitude against celibacy, monasticism, and sexual asceticism. The Prophet Mohammed, himself, has spoken about these subjects as being totally against human nature and harmful to one's health, and he endorses marriage and refrains from promoting sexual austerity. Islamic sexuality is not considered sinful or evil or a sin unless it is illegal and violates the law of chastity:

> And those who do not have the means to get married must keep chaste till Allah provides them the resources by His munificence; and the bondwomen in your possession who, in order to earn something, seek a letter of freedom from you – then write it for them if you consider some goodness in them; and help them in their cause with Allah's wealth which He has bestowed upon you; and do not force your bondwomen into the dirty profession, while they wish to save themselves, in order to earn some riches of the worldly life; and if one forces them then indeed Allah, upon their remaining compelled, is Oft Forgiving, Most Merciful. (Noor 24:33)

Islam also finds that loving desires are the joy of this world, among other things: "Beautified is for mankind the love of these desires - women, and sons, and heaps of gold and piled up silver, and branded horses, and cattle and fields; this is the wealth of the life of this world; and it is Allah, with Whom is the excellent abode." (A/I`mran 3:14)

Unlike Christianity, Islam sees that there is no contradiction between marriage (sex) and worshipping God, though it does consider marriage an advantage in reaching spiritual perfection. As the Prophet says, "He has already guarded half of his religion, therefore he should fear Allah for the other half." (Wasa'il, Vol. 14, p. 5) He also says, "If anyone likes to meet Allah in purity, then he should meet Him with a wife." (Wasa'il, Vol. 14, p 25) These Islamic principles protect against any sexual evolution in the Western meaning of the word, and that is because, as stated by Quran interpreters, originally there was no sexual suppression in Islam.

The Prophet says, "When a man approaches his wife, he is guarded by two angels and [at that moment in Allah's views] he is like a warrior fighting for the cause of Allah. When he has intercourse with her, his sins fell like the leaves of the tree [in fall season]. When he performs the major ablution, he is cleansed from sins." (Wasa'il 'sh-Shi'ah, Vol. 14, p. 74)[115]

The threshold of sexual intercourse that leads to spiritual perfection makes us aware that the Tantric tunnel towards what is more worthy and noble somehow exists in Islam. It holds, too, the duality of delinquency (when illegal) and sanctification (when it "guards half of man's religion"). However, the difference between Islam and Tantra is located in the concept of intercourse, as previously stated in the verses. In Islam, it is a channel to release the sexual yearnings so that the believer can give himself completely to worshipping God. In that exact meaning, intercourse can be an integral part of the process that "leads to the divine self." Nevertheless, this massive amount of examples and texts contained in Hadith and Al-sīra[116] is not intended to dissect the structure of this issue or reveal the mechanism that allows access to spiritual elevation. Although the Kama Sutra explains the techniques of sexual intercourse, some of the old Arabic sex manuals, such as *One Thousand and One Nights*[117] or *The Perfumed Garden of Sensual Pleasures,*[118] may not be considered as such in the technical sense of the word. These books reflect the Arabic, not the Islamic, point of view about the sexual life of women and men, which is not seen the same way by Western critics who mock the status of women in Islam.

The misunderstanding among those critics may not have derived from their dependency on the Islamic and Asian texts or because of a shortage of accurate Islamic references, but because, perhaps, the Quran has come down from, or been revealed by, God in the Arabic language. Arabic culture (language) and religion have become so enmeshed in the minds of outsiders, that many may be surprised to know that several Arab countries have non-Muslim minorities. The particularity of the relationship between these two issues shows that "the Arabic language is one of the first components of the Arab mind and that the Nomad is one of the first components of this language."[119]

The linking between the mind and the language is not only reflected in the theoretical output of philosophers, but in the culture and literature of various peoples—their legends, poetry, and religions.[120] Language that is thought is integrated with the structure of the mind, especially for civilizations or cultures whose developments are based on a holy or semi-sacred book, starting with the Sanskrit Indian civilization, which focused on the Vedas sacred books, through Hellenist civilization, which considered its epic Homeric poetry sacred, all the way to the Arabic and Islamic civilization, in which the Quranic text is the center.[121] In a very inspiring paragraph in Abu Uthman Amr ibn Bahr al-Kinani's ("Al Jahiz")[122] book entitled *Kitab al-Bayan wa al-Tabyin* (*The Book of Eloquence and Oratory*), in which he writes about epiphanies, rhetorical speeches, and sectarian leaders and princes, we find an amazing description of the nature of the Arabic mind. He writes:

> For Arabs, everything is intuitive and improvised from inspiration with no effort or thought; instead they are concerned with speech and the suffering of resurrection's day or pulling up buckets from the well and walking his camel, or Sword duels or dialoguing or fighting or at war…and yet they were

illiterate and unsophisticated. They were capable of poetic, verbal speech and stirring eloquence...."[123]

Although the reference to this description by Al Jahiz goes back to "Arab Jahiliyyah,"[124] as a psychological explanation it shows a certain predisposition which is still present in the structure of the Arab mind: the steady adherence to the beauty of rhetoric, the ability to innovate within it, and the obsessive care of the musical effect that the words leave in the ear.

In fact, the sanctification of the language is completely understood since the revelation of the Quran was revealed by God in the Arabic language as a whole package, which includes truths, theories, axioms, and even scientific facts. Thus, what is left for the Arab is very little. He or she can only put words together to make an endless poetic sentence instead of drafting laws and policies that suit his natural evolution throughout the context of History.

The structure of the Arab mind is very similar to the language it uses. Throughout the ages, this mind was brilliant at improving its linguistic tools and taking the time and effort to safeguard its rules, but at the same time it failed to develop the thought to carry this language. The hidden reason behind this lies in this dangerous and strange conviction: if we develop the thought, this may indicate that we do not agree with the "truth" that is contained in the religious discourse. Well, perhaps Arabs are right to be afraid of developing the thought for the handed down part of their culture, which has been unwavering throughout the ages. As Sāʿid al-Andalusī[125] states in his book Tabaqat al-'Umam,[126] "linguistics, poetry, and rhetoric are the only things that Arabs of Jahiliyyah were proud of and compete with." When Islam came down via divine revelation, Arabs added "knowing Sharia"[127] to this list, and later on medicine that already existed as a science and practice due to the necessity of it, according to Al-Andalusi. As in the time of al-Mansur[128] and his son al-Mammon, the best translators were assigned to Arabize the books of great philosophers such as Plato, Aristotle, Hippocrates, Ptolemy, etc., and thus the Abbasid Dynasty flourished to the degree that it even exceeded the Roman state. However, this period soon faded "due the disruption of the ruling where women and Turks took over. Thus, people gave up education and knowledge and became engaged in struggling until education was about to vanish."[129]

The structure of the Arab mind is an eloquently linguistic one that has nothing to do with philosophy, really, because philosophy and truth have already been monopolized by the sacred text. And any free thinkers who tried to get off the beaten path and use their minds were convicted of heresy because they crossed the forbidden "gates" of the sacred texts. Am I speaking of the features of a contemporary Arab mind somehow?

Again, there may not be a problem with sex in Islam as it is—sex has been recognized as an introduction to "guarding half of the religion," so the problem is located somewhere else. It is in woman, the transitory sex tool for whom the sexual role is not sacred in Islam like it is for man. Her participation in the act of intercourse does not make her "sins fall like the leaves of a tree," or at least there is no reference that ranks her as such.

⚜

In her book *Behind the Veil*, Moroccan feminist and author Fatima Mernissi talks about how love between man and woman threatens the religion of God. The threat, or danger, originates in woman, she says, for being strong and because she is in possession of a sexual energy that is equal to man's. Equality in Islam, she argues, violates the basic principles of the religion because woman is subject to man and therefore she is automatically in a lower position than he is. Her subjection, in that sense, controls her because she is strong and sexually attractive. Inequality here comes from the masculine fear of sexual rivalry because it threatens the security of the Islamic society and pushes it towards a fate of dire consequences.

Woman's image of herself that she sees reflected in her environment's mirror gives her the impression that she is in a lower position because she is the weaker of the two, while man's, or society's, fear of her is actually a fear of her power and strength as a human being and as a sexually and spiritually active person. In addition, her body defies and challenges her "poor" partner, man, who excels in speech, theorizing, and protection while he leaves his life course to God.

The submission of "giving up" to God's command involves a lot of wisdom in a world that is abuzz with arbitrary factors and surprises; nevertheless, it is a mistake to apply the concept of submission to everything. I think this is a hidden trap that makes one unaware of the fact that submission is a singular way to communicate to the Supreme Being, and not to another human, unless it is brought about within a certain pattern of structural and functional hierarchy that preserves his rights and dignity.

The sentimental and sexual "foreplay" with woman, which the prophet Mohammad recommended before intercourse so as to satisfy her prevailing sexual energy and calm her desires, is an acknowledgment to her strong structure and rivalry. Today, unfortunately, foreplay is understood as a test of endurance or an indulgence or even a modern duty that occurs in man's mind as an intellectual, revolutionary leap from the old barbaric ways in which women were approached. Modern man is an educated being who believes in foreplay as if it is a gift for her! He learns that he must "cope" with her and not be in a hurry since this is the character of a "civilized" man, compared to his grandfather who restrained his 13 year-old wife on their wedding night and slapped her twice on the face to render her unconscious, and when she woke up the next day she became a submissive woman.

The culture of foreplay, although it is contained in a religious discourse, was a sign of man's weakness and lack of resourcefulness. Who was she to speak before intercourse? In addition, if he did humor her with foreplay, how would she respond—she who dares not reveal that she is enjoying sex? Fondling him is also dangerous because he speculates that if she knows how to touch him and she enjoys it, then she is a traitor through her sinful knowledge about sex and pleasure.

$$\sim\!\!\sim\!\!\sim$$

A radical change in Muslim society is a huge undertaking, epistemologically speaking. This "ideology" concerning women is stagnant despite the many permanent cultural leaps that have occurred around the world, and which have succeeded, at times, in penetrating the walls of Arab houses. The lack of change is due to the fact that God, so they believe, is the source of this ideology about woman. Fear of woman's sexual power, isolating her, and betraying her with the possibility of replacing her makes it very difficult to imagine an Arabic society that is able to develop itself when the roots of its own transmitted culture run so deep. Perhaps the economic transformations that have taken place have forcibly shaken this inherited discourse and have set the foundations of the social order according to new standards that fit the abilities of the Arab man and woman, their inclinations, and their real existing natures. Moreover, if religious scholars are unable to provide an Islam that is capable of delivering a real and vital image of this religion, an image that fits with the requirements of the present time—and I am certain that this is possible—then this mission should be given to another kind of scholar to accomplish.

Islam is in bad need of a shift in its course, something that has never happened until now.[130] The changes that have been made to the crime and personal status laws were drafted by the force of the political canon and not because of a long, painful struggle with jurisprudence principles. To be authentic, a switch does not mean that we have to change costumes or anything like that as this may simply lock any change into a very narrow and constrictive horizon. A real change should, no matter what, be done on a very high, ethical level.

The dynamics of Islam will still remain a sealed package wrapped with satin and velvet ribbons. An Islamic society that gives precedence to the mind and not to the dogma, unlike the pioneer thinkers in Christianity such as

St. Paul, St. Augustine, and Thomas Aquinas who pushed the mind totally aside in favor of creed, is the most precious gift to the nation. What really matters is an Islam that is willing to see the mind, as Ibn Rushd[131] stated, as coming before doctrine, and to build upon it, for God can be totally revealed by mind.

I am confident that the emergence of Islam as a provoking social and intellectual movement is of the utmost importance to its people. I even consider it creative opposition within this atmosphere. Nevertheless, as the past has allowed Islam to exist as an ideology and religion, then Islam, in its turn, must not accept turning into a static entity of knowledge, but rather remain a permanent and changeable movement. This can be done by giving more freedom to discretion and creation. Obviously, the poem is not more important than the poet is, nor is the photo more important than the photographer, nor is the idea more important than the thinker. It is the poet, the photographer, and the thinker themselves who have created these things in the first place, in much the same way that they create the culture by "making" it with their own hands and minds, and not by simply retrieving, transferring or repeating it.

Too many factors have played a major role in shaping the platform of the Arabic female mind, such as the "concept" of a Polygamist Prophet and the Islamic promise of beautiful women in paradise. Further factors involved in making this platform an active part of the Arabic social milieu, especially in Syria, Lebanon, Jordan, Palestine, and any other Arab country where we find a Christian community, include the image of Christ born to a virgin, the asexual Christian paradise promised in the afterlife, virginity, celibacy, monasticism, and silent avoidance of the sexual stories in the Old Testament. This mental female platform makes up the "truth" of the sacred discourse in which she doesn't even have a say.

Apparently, ours is a culture of silent and blindfolded "legitimate" violence with a great deal of bleeding wounds.

The Culture of Legitimate Violence

"Legitimate violence" is an expression that opens the floodgates to endless questions and speculations, not only about woman, but also about the Arab world today. We entered the millennium with this kind of justified violence in general, so brutality against woman, perhaps, seems to be the softest and the most bearable amongst all.

Due to "anti-terrorism" laws, which were enacted to fight terrorism, our world has witnessed too many massacres where, in some countries, millions of people have been victimized by it. Human bodies and spirits have been sentenced to death, intentionally or unintentionally, without any trial at all and justifications were spouted, one after the other, to excuse the uncivilized violations against men and women alike.

Strangely enough, there have been philosophies and perspectives that have contributed to some of these abuses by sterilizing them with examples and proofs of legitimacy.

In fact, to some "believers," it is acceptable and justifiable to kill a whole neighborhood with explosives just because they feel that this action may contribute to their ultimate "noble" goal. Some others find it logical to treat woman according to the popular Arabic proverbs: "woman is like a carpet, she needs a flick every now and then," or "woman is like a green olive, her oil becomes delicious by squeezing," or "woman is like a doorknob, she is permissible for all hands at all times." And their religious pretext is always: this is God's order.

The dispute here is located somewhere beyond complaints or the available studies and statistics of the United Nations about violence around the world and especially in the Arab world. There is an obvious difficulty in doing surveys and assessing the exact number of incidents of legitimate violence that are tolerated by some Arabic social decrees. The reason this debate lies outside all these boundaries is, in my opinion, due the mindset of the violent person, or the suppressor—whether man or woman. Violence and repression are two sides of the same coin in the fabric of the violent individual. They manifest in his destructive tendency, and in the fact that he is an anti-social personality who finds his permission in the most destructive and distorted written or verbal laws of society.

The cultural level of the suppressor doesn't have much to do with improving the behavior of the violent person, but rather makes his tools more creative and sophisticated. "Harem virus,"[132] for example, affects many educated men after marriage, whereas we may find an illiterate man with a constructive and advanced personality. Therefore, statistics by themselves do not play an essential role in disciplining the personality unless he or she is originally sane and ethical without harmful and defensive reactions toward others and his or her environment.

The creative geniality of Nietzsche did not prevent him from admitting his belief that "woman has much reason for shame; so much pedantry, superficiality, schoolmarmishness, petty presumption, petty licentiousness and immodesty lies concealed in woman."[133] Nor did it prevent theologian St. Thomas from saying that "if it were not for some [divine] power that wanted the feminine sex to exist, the birth of a woman would be just another accident, such as that of other monsters [i.e., a dog with two heads, a calf with five legs, etc.]."[134] And not even Aristotle's philosophical mind could stop him from believing that "females are weaker and colder in nature, and we must look upon the female character as being a sort of natural deficiency"[135] nor Plato's intelligence from assuring us "the relation of male to female is by nature a relation of superior to inferior and ruler to ruled."[136] Finally, even Tawfiq Al-hakim[137] could not help himself from judging that "beauty is the only excuse for one to forgive all woman's vanity and foolishness."

If such respected thinkers have written and said these negative statements about woman, then there must be some specific characteristic in the type of person who launches these kinds of proverbs into the popular lexicon—and all with the plainest of languages, free of any linguistic sophistication or rhetoric.

Isn't it considered violence when the Arabic political mind sees all Arab citizens as copies, mere sheep? Isn't it considered violence when the Arabic social mind sees that the Arab man's dignity and honor are completely located in his "harem" rather than his conscience, work values, or achievements? Is it not considered violent when the Arabic religious mind assumes that the newborn does not need to ask questions or leave the family house so he can proceed with his own life away from the "big house of the orthodox culture," i.e. society and religion? Is it not considered violent when our Arabic culture forces those who dare look outside the cultural window or "complain to the bricks of the ground," as the popular Egyptian proverb says, to atone?

All these are silent but violent gestures that are happening all the time.

However, this violent state of mind is not, in fact, collective cultural folklore, but rather an individual "personality" who has specific characteristics and, moreover, is the one who drafts the laws and issues the decrees of

"Haram and Halal."[138]

Many examples in history show, in their iconic features, the model for the individual who exerts a "silent and legitimate violence" against others, regardless of the nature of this violence, whether cultural, economic, political, religious, social, or sexual.

The media, for instance, is not "something" but rather "somebody" who manages the news in such a way that increases his income and "sells" more by spreading the violent and suppressive data around in order to control people with fear. It is amazing what the media can do during wars because news media, to quite a large degree, function independently and without rules or even any ethical codes, aside from a few that are self-imposed.

This gigantic tool (the media) is controlling the masses not only via bad news but also via broad and faltering statements. For example, when the Western media wants to demonize some Middle Eastern leader, it alters the truth about him, his life, his family, his supporters, and his activities. This is not only the definition of "rumor," but is also the structure of the silent violence that relies upon very vague, inadequate, and broad statements. It's the same thing when we talk about the "person" who circulates proverbs with their painful and broad judgments that include every person in the society or group of people. Some proverbs about mothers-in-law, for example, are extremely harmful and do not mean specific women but simply encompass all mothers-in-law in one general, and usually negative, evaluation.

Since the media primarily doles out bad news in order to control the masses and tell its story in a way that makes its supporters (i.e. the government or the country as a whole) "win" the war and increase its income, then how, for God's sake, will it convey any good news about something or somebody?

People feel threatened around this kind of media or proverb, which is an excellent way to keep them obedient and submissive. And what does the media provide the nation with? What is the proverbs' final product? What is the purpose behind this large number of degrading beliefs in the collective unconscious about woman that discards her, scorns her, shuns her, and even kills her? It is just pure, silent violence in order to control the masses. War is good for the media's business and proverbs are good for the mind-shaping of society.

Strangely enough, it is a hidden fear of the "other," which lies within the media's approach and the folkloric proverbs—or, to be more specific, the person who monitors the "game"—that drives them to invent a whole world full of lies and imagined threats. To such a person, every human being is an enemy that he needs to get rid of either secretly or openly. I offer the example of Hitler who did not want to reveal too much about himself.

"In 1930, he brought his nineteen year-old nephew Patrick, whom he had never met before, to Munich where he told him never to grant interviews to the press: "You idiots". He shouted, *you're going to do me in. People must not know who I am. They must not know where I come from and who my family is. Not even in my book did I allow one word to come out about these things. I am an entirely nonfamilial being. I only belong to my folkish community.*" (Haman, p. 51) Adolf Hitler was a secretive man. Hardly any prominent figure in history has ever tried so hard to cover his tracks."[139]

The survival of Hitler depended on keeping others in a state of ignorance. He believed that he was doing everything for the benefit of his people and their salvation. He felt threatened; therefore he had to put everyone in his state down.

"He disliked most of his teachers because *they had no sympathy with youth: their one objective was stuff our brains and turn us into erudite apes like themselves.*' His French teacher, Dr. Huemer, testified at his trial in 1924: He was decidedly gifted, if one-sided, but had difficulty controlling his temper. He was considered intractable and willful, always had to be right and easily flew off the handle, and he clearly found it difficult to accommodate himself to the limits of a school. He demanded unconditional subordination from his schoolmates. (Haman, p. 11)" [140]

Hitler is an example of the individual who can fantasize about and generate such proverbs and media and of course who could easily create the Haremlik. His feeling of danger and fright is disguised and cryptic to the point where it is sometimes difficult to distinguish his violent tendency. He even appears very logical and convincing: the essential part of his charisma and glamorous insanity.

※ ※ ※

Let us pay attention to some of the facts in this regard. The sexual violence perpetrated by soldiers during armed conflicts is something both known and in vogue. This does not mean that every battalion or soldier has, without exception, violent or suppressive characteristics, but rather there are certain conditions that the individual finds himself in so that he reacts in a particular way.

Statistics contained in the 2006 in-depth study "Ending Violence Against Women: From Words to Action" by the Secretary-General of the United Nations shows terrifying facts regarding this type of "traditional and, apparently, legitimate" violence that occurs in periods of armed conflict. Under a section entitled "Violence Against Women in Armed Conflict" it says:

During armed conflict, women experience all forms

157

of physical, sexual and psychological violence perpetrated by both State and non-State actors. These forms include murder, unlawful killings, torture and other cruel, inhuman or degrading treatment or punishment, abductions, maiming and mutilation, forced recruitment of women combatants, rape, sexual slavery, sexual exploitation, involuntary disappearance, arbitrary detention, forced marriage, forced prostitution, forced abortion, forced pregnancy and forced sterilization.... Sexual violence has been used during armed conflict for many different reasons, including as a form of torture, to inflict injury, to extract information, to degrade and intimidate and to destroy communities. Rape of women has been used to humiliate opponents, to drive communities and groups off land and to willfully spread HIV..... Violence against women has been reported from conflict or post-conflict situations in many countries or areas including Afghanistan, Burundi, Chad, Colombia, Côte d'Ivoire, Democratic Republic of the Congo, Liberia, Peru, Rwanda, Sierra Leone, Chechnya/Russian Federation, Darfur, Sudan, northern Uganda and the former Yugoslavia.[141]

The violent person is not aware of the fact that he is

being violent. Only the individual who has a well-balanced mind can objectively see his own behavior.

It is wise to take into consideration the characteristics of the violent person so that they become part of society's knowledge about human behavior and patterns. In knowing this data, such a person is not likely to be assigned a leading position, whether political, social, administrative or executive.

❦

Popular memory is an integrated ideological basket. It is also a highly-sensitive lens that continuously monitors, photographs, and records everything that has to do with human beings spiritually, mentally, and physically from their first appearance on earth to the present day. This lens is a clear and unmerciful mirror. Although it looks soulless, due to the rigid precision of its images and words, the popular memory is a panoramic tape that consists of thoughts, proverbs, anecdotes, assumptions, literature, art, culture, architectural heritage, science, mythology, ethics, profane beliefs and rituals, and customs of every kind. On this tape, we also see the story of the evolution of languages and communication that is loaded with all the social, religious, and political rules that we can imagine. This memory is a huge pot that contains all types of men and women, the history of all ethnic cuisines, fashions, art, war, the development of agriculture and industry, the anatomy of love and hate, the human tonal scale, suppressed dreams, the dramatized agonies of prophets, the victorious "hurrahs" of politicians, and fleeting joy. Popular memory is a giant closet made up of histrionic battles led by military generals, leaders, heroes, legislators, and rulers braided with wreaths of suffering and glory on their heads. It is also a very old closet for poor people's shreds of clothing and the holy veils of women throughout history. It contains the painful history of woman's "delaying of the sunset" as well as the festive Harem and everything that is related to it, such as proverbs, stories, laws, and practices.

Although the popular memory is not an informative history of a people in the conventional sense, its effect is very similar to the media today, though in a slower rhythm and with a more comprehensive range of movement. Regardless of the fact that a new "memory," or culture, is emerging continuously in society, so that the popular memory looks deficient somehow, the impact of this memory on the civic culture is so "factual" that almost no one verifies or examines it. Thus, this memory quietly sneaks into the fabric of the individual's mind and spirit with education and verbal transmission, generation after generation.

The difference between the popular civic culture and any other indoctrinated culture is that the popular culture is naturally linked to the process of temporal and spatial movement of history, i.e. it is the product of class, generation, creed, and "means of production"[142] conflict. This culture has grown away from the religious culture that enveloped man, not only because of some specific intellectual or materialistic conflict, but also because it was taught to him in the form of unquestionable divine decrees. Consequently, we have two kinds of cultures at hand: the civic-popular culture, which is the animated, active, and reactive one, and the religious culture, which is the stable, fixed, and well-established one.

It is interesting to note that the popular civic culture was once mystically religious. Both women and men have contributed to this evolution by broadcasting it widely through chatter and gossip, as well as by supporting its abnormal educational texts. This influence is shown clearly at home when parents encourage the big brother to discipline his sister, or the husband to beat up his wife, or do not allow the woman to run her life financially, and other systems of violence in the form of continuous verbal and physical insults, belittling her or isolating her and so forth.

In this chapter, I will go over some of the common Arabic proverbs in order to study, in accordance with the annual reports of the United Nations, the widespread phenomenon of legitimate violence against woman, which is another form of discrimination based on her gender.

Popular Proverbs and the Physical Violence Against Woman

Proverbs do not contain all types of legitimate and non-legitimate physical violence that is currently practiced against women. However, some of these types are developed by circumstances, or perhaps by social and intellectual developments, or even by the vitality of cultural movement that is commensurate with the temporal and spatial process of history and with the means of production, as I mentioned earlier.

Arabic proverbs such as "beat your woman before lunch and after dinner," "girls are either buried or married," "shame caused by woman is only washed away by blood," "woman's death is blessed," "woman is like a carpet, she needs a flick every now and then," "do not enter a woman's house without a whip," and "it is a joy when a baby girl dies when born," are clear examples that illustrate the pervasiveness of popular violence, which is preserved in the memory of the society, and perhaps in the existing roots of all forms of violence that women suffer from today.

These proverbs document the legitimacy of disdaining women and establishing her inferiority. They also expose the structural imbalance in inequality between "her" and "him." Today, the concept of physical violence against women seems more variable and almost without boundaries; it includes domestic and social violence, as well as the violence perpetrated or condoned by the state. There are certain categories of women that are particularly vulnerable to legitimate violence, including "minority, indigenous and refugee women, destitute women, women in institutions or in detention, girls, women with disabilities, older women and women in situations of armed conflict."[143]

In fact, the gender-based violence "is generated by sociocultural attitudes and cultures of violence in all parts of the world, and especially by norms about the control of female reproduction and sexuality."[144] Furthermore, "violence against women intersects with other factors, such as race and class, and with other forms of violence, including ethnic conflict."[145]

It seems that no single cause adequately accounts for violence against women, although the violent scene has "the convergence of specific factors within the broad context of power inequalities at the individual, group, national and global levels."[146] Hence, "factors such as women's race, ethnicity, caste, class, migrant or refugee status, age, religion, sexual orientation, marital status, disability or HIV status will influence what forms of violence they suffer and how they experience it."[147]

Popular Proverbs and the Emotional and Psychological Violence Against Woman

These proverbs assign negative qualities to woman in order to belittle her or provide a warning about her to the point that some proverbs compare her quite frankly to the devil or to animals. These "violent concepts" about woman have actually entered into the fabric of society's general understanding of emotional and verbal violence against her. This type of violence is the most prevalent and legitimate of all, because it is an "on-demand" type of violence, ready for delivery without any delay, and has its own justifications, terms, legitimacy, and destructive proverbs. Here we can smell the stink of gender-based discrimination at its peak, as well as see the hierarchy of power and the dependency on an ideological and material basis, for "patriarchy has been entrenched in social and cultural norms, institutionalized in the law and political structures and embedded in local and global economies. It has also been ingrained in formal ideologies and in public discourse."[148]

The first proverb comes out of woman's own lips: "Shout at me but do not beat me with a raspberry branch." This means that she prefers to die than to be humiliated or subject to any kind of violence. Among all the proverbs, which number in the hundreds, I mention the following: "Trust a snake, but do not trust a woman." This means that woman is not trustworthy and cannot keep a secret. "Do not obey your woman, otherwise you will be regretful." This means that man is capable of handling his own life without her help or advice. "Woman shares her half-mind with Satan." This is "evidence" of the sneaky and evil mind of woman. "Woman's house is her only tomb." This means that the marital home is also the graveyard for woman who has nothing else. "A girl is a broken wing" means that woman is powerless and cannot run her life by herself. The list is endless because we are afraid to look at this verbally violent heritage without any disciplinary law to prevent it or a genuine political desire to stop the mockery of woman that veils arrogance and contempt.

Oddly enough, for every step of progress made to empower woman, there is strong resistance to change the socio-cultural attitudes that tolerate violence perpetrators. When the state fails to condemn these people, it is sending a message to the community that masculine violence against woman is something acceptable and legitimate. Thus, this violent behavior becomes normal and a standard pattern. "There are certain cultural norms that have long been cited as causal factors for violence against women, including the beliefs associated with 'harmful traditional practices' (such as female genital mutilation/cutting, child marriage and son preference), crimes committed in the name of 'honor,' discriminatory criminal punishments imposed under religiously based laws, and restrictions on women's rights in marriage."[149]

According to the in-depth study "Ending Violence Against Women: From Words to Action" by the UN Secretary-General, some organized political forces, including different forms of cultural or religious "fundamentalism," have put pressure on governments to *reverse* advances in women's rights. This means that previous gains by women have been eroded or are under threat in some countries around the world. Hence, these religious fundamentalists are obstacles in discerning the exact data and statistics about violence against women. A shortage of data may hinder the understanding of this ongoing phenomenon, as well as further studies and analysis that would be based upon it.

It is important to realize that "cultural relativist arguments have been advanced in national contexts and in international debates when laws and practices that curtail women's human rights have been challenged. The politicization of culture in the form of religious fundamentalisms in diverse geographic and religious contexts has become a serious challenge to efforts to secure women's human rights."[150]

Moreover, ten years after its creation, the United Nations Trust Fund to End Violence Against Women only receives less than $2 million a year, as if it is a tacit admission that the money should be spent on other, more important, things than woman's welfare, whom proverbs classify as the "devil" or as only having "half a mind."

Popular Proverbs and Economic Violence Against Woman

Economic inequalities can be a causal factor for violence against women both at the level of individual acts of violence and at the level of broad-based economic trends that create or exacerbate the enabling conditions for such violence.[151]

Through a simple examination on a global level for this argument, we find that rich countries suppress those who are less fortunate and developed by trying to control their resources, dominate them, and mandate them politically and economically. Good economic power means the ability to make decisions and the independence that results from these decisions. Using the same argument, we find that "women's economic inequalities and discrimination against her in areas such as employment, income, access to other economic resources and lack of economic independence reduces women's capacity to act and make decisions, and increases their vulnerability to violence."[152]

The economic exploitation of women starts with the family, in the Arabic states, as she is denied access to and control over basic resources. Thus, she is not in a position to possess or manage the family's finances, including personal property, without which makes her vulnerable, dependent, and subject to violence. In marginalized communities, privatization and globalization of the public sector leads to perpetuating gender inequality on both economic and social levels.

If national governments were able to promote women's rights in the past by way of public sector policy support and social programs, it is no longer the case when new policies are brought about, as their actions are deliberately built on structural adjustment programs and reorganization of the economy according to very different foundations. Globalization increases the gap between the rich and the poor with all the social pressures and disparity that may emerge, and creates new patterns of violence against women, including illegal trafficking, just like what happened after the collapse of the former Soviet Union. Perhaps the masculine labor laws today are the most violent and legitimate trap to which the modern economy has given birth. Woman, like man, is under unmerciful pressure and is just another "individual" who lives in the globalization era, a human being that is imprisoned between the hammer and anvil of the existing laws.

Arabic popular memory is filled with proverbs and parables that insist on the inability of women to control economic resources, or to understand the principle of money. The most revealing and ironic among these proverbs is "woman's income is spent on make-up only." In other words, woman is incapable of managing her financial life. "For her adornments, woman borrows money" indicates that she is so interested in herself that she is willing to borrow money in order to satisfy her beautification needs. "Woman is concerned with a man's pocket and not his sins" shows that woman worries only about money. "There are two things you should not give your woman: your money and your secrets." This means that woman is incapable of her household's financial management.

Men control the family wealth, i.e. the economic resources, and are the sole decision-makers and authority, which tends to increase the probability of violence towards woman. Poor economic conditions may force the whole family, including wives, children, aunts, brothers, etc., to live together in one house, which unfortunately creates an emotional climate that is more prone to violence and viciousness because of the physical claustrophobia and increase in daily confrontations and frustrations.

Popular Proverbs and Domestic Violence
(Honor Crimes)

This is one of the most common kinds of violence

worldwide that occurs among married couples or otherwise intimate relationships. A 2005 study in the Syrian Arab Republic[153] revealed that 21.8 percent of women have experienced some form of violence in the family and of these, 48 percent have been beaten.[154] Within the scope of this type of violence, we are familiar with acts such as abusive sexual contact, making a woman engage in a sexual act without her consent, and attempted or completed sex acts with a woman who is ill, disabled, under pressure, or under the influence of alcohol or other drugs.[155] Hence, acts such as "intimidation and aggressive yelling, slander, threats, humiliation and psycho-terror, female infanticide and prenatal sex selection, early marriage, dowry-related violence, female genital mutilation/cutting, crimes against women committed in the name of 'honor,' maltreatment of widows, including inciting widows to commit suicide, are forms of violence against women that are considered harmful traditional practices, and may involve both family and community."[156] In the same category of domestic violence, there are also "restrictions on a second daughter's right to marry, dietary restrictions for pregnant women, forced feeding and nutritional taboos, marriage to a deceased husband's brother and witch hunts."[157]

Among domestic crimes, this is the most "legitimate" and most harmful, and attracts the most attention; not all honor crimes are reported, and thus not documented. UNFPA estimated that 50,000 women are murdered by family members each year in "honor killings" around the world.[158]

One may be surprised to find the seeds of this kind of domestic incitement and violence in proverbs, as well as exaggeration and humor, or even sarcasm, as if to promote the "legitimacy" of the incitement and its implementation. Hence, this legitimacy paves the way for approval, and approval is the basis of the suppressive judgments that form the substantive fabric of such folk. This ironic humor allows the violence to extend its multiple arms in all directions like an octopus; it is there on public transportation, in workplaces, schools, sports clubs, colleges, hospitals, and religious and other social institutions. Here are some proverbs in that regard, to mention just a few:

"Cut the cat's throat in your wedding day" means make your wife feel your strength from the beginning. "What a joy, my sister got married" means that a woman's older sister got married and now she may as well. "If you do not want your daughter to get married, just increase her dowry." This proverb refers to the denial of woman's self-determinism as far as the marriage decision is concerned. "Woman's luck is like a watermelon" indicates that women do not know anything about their future husbands since they are not allowed to see or talk to him before marriage. "If you want to safeguard your honor, then let your daughter marry the one she loves" points out that being single and in love is unacceptable and may lead to scandal and gossip within the family and community, and therefore the best thing to do is to handle this by marriage. "If a young girl is saved from shame (by being married), then she will bring the enemy into the house." The enemy here is the son-in-law who will request his share of his wife's legacy. "Marry off your daughter before your son" is a "must" in order to shield her dignity and honor. "A girl's honor is like a matchstick, it ignites once" is the proverb that most Arab drama has been built upon when addressing a serious female issue such as losing her virginity and so forth.

On the other hand, popular culture gives man the favored status and preference when it insists that "man is like a horse, and he is not disadvantaged by anything...but his pocket," which means that man is strong enough to do whatever he wants as long as his pocket is full of money. "When man commits adultery, he becomes like a lustrous sword." As for this proverb, God knows what the cultural background is that allows this kind of proverb to be disseminated in the first place!

Violence that is Not Documented in Proverbs

There are many forms of violence that are conservatively undocumented in popular memory or proverbs, all based on disdaining and belittling woman, and are considered semi-sacred. Actually, these undocumented forms of violence are committed by "State agents including all people empowered to exercise elements of State authority—members of the legislative, executive and judicial branches, as well as law enforcement officials, social security officials, prison guards, officials in places of detention, immigration officials and military and security forces."[159] It is manifested in the form of "torture acts, degrading treatment or sexual harassment and molestation. A State may also perpetrate violence against women through its laws and policies. Examples of such laws and policies comprise those that criminalize women's consensual sexual behavior as a means to control women; policies on forced sterilization, forced pregnancy and forced abortion; policies on protective custody of women that effectively imprisons them; and other laws and policies including policies on virginity testing and sanctioning forced marriages, that fail to recognize women's autonomy and agency and legitimize male control over women. States may also condone violence against women through inadequate laws or through ineffective implementation of laws, effectively allowing perpetrators of violence against women impunity for their acts."[160] Other forms of violence against women in custody that have been documented by various sources include: inappropriate surveillance during showers or undressing;

strip searches conducted by or in the presence of men; and verbal sexual harassment.[161]

The "explicit" suggestion to kill a woman is not documented in popular proverbs, although the encouragement and levity of it is implicitly stated in the words, as illustrated by the proverb that declares, "What a joy if a newborn girl died the moment she was born." There are no proverbs that encourage the trafficking of women for sexual purposes, or other exploitations such as acid throwing, stalking, or distorting part of her body, and neither are there any proverbs that document violence associated with ethnic minorities, women with disabilities, or the sexual exploitation of migrant women or maids. Nevertheless, "folkloric killing," so to speak, is associated with its passionate feature rather than its intentional criminal sense, i.e. this violence may happen because of excessive jealousy and overwhelming love or deep longing. Or, as some proverbs describe it, "when a woman is beaten by her lover, it is like she is eating raisins," "love is blind," or "love is a killer"!

The Psychological Attitude of Haremlik's Architect

There is a so-called "affectionate" form of legitimate violence against women, and it is imprisoning her within the walls of the Haremlik. As defined in one of the footnotes in Fatima Mernissi's important book *Dreams of*

Trespass: Tales of a Harem Girlhood, Haremlik is divided into two types, domestic and imperial, the latter of which is filled with maids like Herron al-Rashid's Haremlik. As for the domestic type, it is a courtyard occupied by wives, aunts, daughters, nieces, maids, and small boys that is encircled by high walls.

The imperial harem is the one that inflamed the imagination of the Orientalists. We find it in the works of Western artists in the eighteenth and nineteenth centuries, where paintings are packed with women who freely smoke water pipes in Haremliks that are fabulously furnished with emasculated boys, Ottoman swords, Persian carpets, and Brocade cloths. It is the mysterious Eastern royal prison, or, to be more precise, the official and legitimate female prison of the Arab world.

The domestic Haremlik seems more insulting and painful, and less fantastic and sensual, than the imperial one. It is the Haremlik of separation or veiling, and not necessarily one of polygamy or of "emptiness within," as Mernissi says, where women are completely excluded from the outside world of men. It is legitimate violence in its utmost symbolic sense that is directed against woman where man is both the "victim" and the executioner.

Man, as well, lives in a cruel isolation away from "woman." He is the architect of her Haremlik and thinks that what he is doing is "for the good of others," an expression that he repeats constantly. He feels that he is the only good and right person in his surroundings. He believes that he is an expert on how to make people happy, and therefore he is a great decision maker for the benefit of all. However, his conduct is based on the following analysis: if everyone drops dead (or becomes imprisoned or isolated), no one can threaten him or protect him against his own foolish imagination. In fact, he is obsessed with protecting himself and his survival, and the Haremlik is one of his ideas of how to do this.

Such an individual at the helm of a nation, for example, may turn the entire country into a huge Haremlik closed in by "protective" walls. Entire civilizations, such as Egypt, Babylon, Rome, and Russia, to name a few, have collapsed because they were ruled by oppressive kings and leaders.

I think it is time for us to understand that when things are run properly, it is not because man is good or scared, but simply because of his ability to carry matters out properly and humanely. Violence is not a circumstance, a situation, or a condition; it comes from a person.

Legitimate Violence in Cinematic Drama

At the beginning of the nineteenth century, scientists discovered a phenomenon for which they have not yet found an explanation: the complex process of vision. If one develops a set of consecutive, still images and runs through them in sequence, one sees them as if they are actually moving. This strange experience is called "the persistence of vision phenomenon," which means that even after the physical image disappears, the image endures in the mind. This is called "positive image" and is the principle of animation.

The trap that the mind finds itself in, regarding these consecutive images, is seeing them move so fast and in such a way that it is unable to analyze what is going on exactly, and thus the simplest explanation is to believe that the images are actually moving.

When we see a scene of a man hitting a woman for thirty seconds in a movie, this means that there are 24 frames, or images, per second to produce the hitting motion. In other words, there are 720 reflected images on the screen, and between each image there is a fraction of a second of darkness. If the words "good morning" need 20-22 frames for an actor to move his lips, then a physical blow needs much more. And we call this, in terms of motion picture technique, a "positive image"!

In fact, there is so much more to that, for what is "positive" at a technical level may be "negative" as far as cinematic drama is concerned. There is a great difference between the technical tendency for artistic perfection and the hidden tendencies of drama. A technically successful blow could be a failure at a dramatic level unless it is very well handled and invested in the movie's story, although I doubt the ability of drawing lessons about the disadvantages of violence through violent scenes shown in all its "realistic" details.

Some directors and writers have another point of view. Under the pretext of "realism in drama," many violent scenes have been produced with great exaggeration,[162] time after time, turning movie and television screens into a "school" that teaches such violence. Needless to say, there is a role that American movies play in promoting such violence, as the United Nations admits that eighty percent of women are murdered by their intimate partners. These crimes are inspired by the violent drama that constantly plays around them, day and night.

It is remarkable that violence in American movies, impressively spread to most of the Arab world (not that we need lessons in violence), is based on a retaliation template. This template, well known to those who write for such movies, comprises a hero who sees himself as the law when he decides to take revenge for his loved one. This is what we call "violence in the name of law" and is so popular now in movies in the West that the national hero is actually rewarded and crowned for this wreckage of legitimate and "legal" violence. This shows how dangerous the effect that drama, whether positive or negative, has on human awareness.

In fact, there is a fundamental difference between a novelist and screenwriter. The latter has to have a fertile imagination, a strong visual sense, and a very competent ability in writing convincing scenes. For instance, if a novelist writes "Ahmed beats up his wife every day," this sentence may not have as powerful an effect on the reader as a cinematic, visual scene of a wife being furiously beaten up by her husband. Such a scene, when "professionally" done in a movie, allows us to watch and feel what appears to be real violence, complete with a lover who angrily whips his woman, with an object or his fist, while she screams and struggles, her clothes ripped and tears in her eyes.

The trick to filmic drama is its ability to reproduce the identity, both self-identity and the identity of the community, through dialogue. Eighteenth-century novels and other behavioral pattern books—as per American critic Nancy Armstrong in her excellent work titled *How Novels Think: The Limits of Individualism 1719-1900*[163]—have contributed to "producing" the modern individual. This is a person whose identity and values originate from his personal feelings and characteristics, rather than his status within the social hierarchy. This perception of identity is supported today by movie scenarios, television series, and print and TV ads, all of which keep us informed about what it means to be a man or a woman.[164]

Today, drama engages the viewer with dialogue in ways that require a lot of assimilation with the characters and their actions. This assimilation is what creates identity. We become who we are through integration with other people when we read their works, listen to them talk, and watch their attitudes and reactions. If the recipient has the characteristics of a violent and suppressive person, then it is enough for him to see violence in order for the whole world around him to bloom.

The mechanism of integration, or assimilation, is the most serious of all. It is a precious responsibility that is in the hands of our writers, photographers, actors, and filmmakers, which requires a great degree of wisdom and ethics to handle.

Identity, which is formed by assimilation, may be false when it is shaped on the "realism" that good screenwriting imparts on the characters and impacts the receiver. I have a friend who suffered from this dilemma when she was avidly reading Paulo Coelho's novel *Eleven Minutes*, which is about a woman who becomes, through her life events, a prostitute. The writing is so good and the dramatic motives of the protagonist are drawn so accurately and aesthetically, that prostitution seemed completely justifiable to my friend. Well, whoever said that words are double-edged swords was totally right.

More accurately, an identity that is formed by integration is an incomplete one, to a certain degree, because it doesn't allow a person to reach the type of happiness that he normally feels when he is his authentic self and living his own personal and intellectual experiences.

Thus, the "I" of the human being today does not evolve freely anymore—or maybe at anytime—in a world where irresponsible and negative drama occupies a huge part of our vision of this world. If visual media is offering us stereotyped outfits, ways of speech, attitudes, food, and social considerations regarding many of our human activities, then it's not hard to understand the degree to which this person is unfamiliar with the authentic identity of a human being. And this is the difference between writing prose and writing for movies.

Even the horrific statistics and studies on violence that are heavily loaded with frightening statements, prepared by the United Nations and civil society organizations, do not have the same impact on us as moving pictures do. So shouldn't writers and filmmakers pay attention to each uttered or written word, and each action their characters make in the movies? Isn't it necessary for those people to have a constructive cultural project that stems from the real needs of society so as to avoid promoting violence, drugs, and negative values in their films? I put this question to you, dear reader.

⚜

Motive is what drives every human being in this world. Everything we do is because of the motivation of getting or receiving the thing we want. We eat because we are hungry, we learn because we need to be an expert in the field, i.e. get a job, we work because we need the money to survive, and so on.

If we write about a man's violent action against a woman he knows, then the most basic element in treating this "story" as a novel or a movie is to find the motivation of or justification for this behavior. Arabic drama portrays woman as a superficial human being, even when she is playing the role of president. She is a belly dancer, a naïve mother, a traitor, a prostitute, or any kind of instigator of nonsense. She is weak and fragile in her femininity, and her ignorance is the justification for the "dramatic" violence towards her. Bad drama tends to, knowingly or unknowingly, "adorn blindness," i.e. make violence look shiny and acceptable.

There are two other things that Arabic dramas take into account when legitimizing, both publicly and covertly, pretexts to "adorn blindness," and these are market need and profit. The truth is that there is a reciprocal relationship between these two terms because there would be no profit if the market need was not satisfied and vice versa. The market need is the source that secures the profit, and always according to the devotees of the contemporary visual drama.

❧

Covert violence lies in the rules that govern a big part of artistic and cinematic life. It manifests itself in the following facts:

1. Man is getting the largest share of the influential and key roles.

2. Distortion of woman's image in drama is another discrimination feature, where sex, including verbal and physical excitement, occupies the majority of her roles. She is given the part of unfaithful wife or partner, menial girlfriend, drug user, prostitute, or helpless mother. There have been many studies done by the Centre for Media Research at the University of Cairo which acknowledge that 72 percent of female cinematic characters embody very negative attributes, such as alcohol addiction, the promotion of sins, and the use of profanity, and always do so within satirical comedy plots so as to help the rapid expansion of the show, and thus the enhancement of moral deterioration. Such images of women's nature in cinema is one of the most widespread forms of

legitimate violence and has a huge impact on the audience.

3. Arabic dramas still avoid any kind of deep discussion on topics such as female honor, by which I mean woman's freedom to control anything that has to do with her body in the way that she wants. Honor is one of the core themes in Arabic society that justifies violence against women.

   Arabs have been unwilling to handle this controversial topic of separating man's honor from woman's behavior in the cinema, fearing that this may open the floodgates for other unpredictable ideas such as shaking up the religious vernacular of a community. Honor and dignity lie deeply in (1) respecting the natural laws, and (2) adopting a transparent attitude toward the world, life, and human beings, and not in hiding a woman's legs.

4. Promoting these fragile types of women as models for femininity, or femininity as it should be, is dangerous. The title of "First Lady of the Arabic Screen" that was publicly offered to Egyptian actress Faten Hamama is the equivalent of "National Hero," a title given to man by Western cinema for portraying his sex in an "attractive" manner. Both models are there for us to replicate and are the icons of both their eras and their genders.

Faten Hamama, an acclaimed actress of film and television, has carried this "title" competently for her fantastic performing capabilities. She is the most honored actress in the Middle East and one of the pioneering women who persevered persistently throughout her career to develop her talent and devote herself only to quality roles free from degrading sexual impurities. This was quite an amazing feat, knowing that her movies did not match the so-called "what the public wants" theory.

Nevertheless, through her roles as a subjugated girl who is always exposed to injustice and aggression, she has weakened the image of the able and free woman, and has promoted, unknowingly perhaps, woman's negative fragility and tenderness that instigate violence against her. Later on, these qualities became the ideal scene of "woman with a complete femininity."

During the era of her youth, Faten Hamama's first films such as *The Small Millionaire* and *Angel of Mercy* (where she was an angel, a light from the sky) were not worthy enough to be stopped by. Those roles were limited to the smart and sweet girl who uses humor and brains in a nice way to approach life and others. Then she entered the stage of romantic movies where she excelled at playing the role of a young lady who is in love but also a victim of poor living conditions and suffocating social dilemmas, and whose only goal is to find the love of her life and marry him.

Examples include *Pity My Tears, Immortality, The Unjust Angel, Our Beautiful Days, Love and Tears,* and *Among the Ruins.* Finally, Hamama gave up the roles of an angel girl to enter a new era of weeping roles, and once again, she embodied the character of a poor girl who struggles with her destiny and is unable to get along because of her fragility and weakness. Even the victory of the "good" ending does not happen by her self-effort, but rather by the intervention of divine providence and chance, so she is personally safe as "part of the whole package of victory."

The shortage of good roles at that stage of her career paved the way for the iconic image of the fragile and tormented girl to become ideal fodder for all kinds of violence and suppression from others—and amazingly this was attractive to the public!

Although her later roles as an evil woman in *Sleepless,* a commando in *God Is With Us,* and a liberal progressive in *The Barred Road* were quite atypical, these were the exceptions in her career, calling to mind the proverb "a flower does not make a spring."

In a subsequent period of her life as an actress, Hamama focused on topics that dealt with the problems of the Egyptian family in such films as *Housewife, Every Family Has a Head, The Empire of M,* and *I Want a Solution.* Although she was able to give voice to some very important issues in these movies, such as freedom and personal status laws related to divorce, she still remained that fragile and weak type who suffers in front of the barricades of social, legal, and religious issues. Even her movie *Mouths and Rabbits*, which caused a huge sensation at the time, can be summarized to a simple love story that is troubled by differences between the lovers.

Hamama's iconic place in the history of the Egyptian movie industry has promoted the romantic model throughout Arabic societies. In fact, she did not offer much to Egyptian or Arabic women who were living their own hell of Haremlik. Despite her long history in the cinema (over 100 movies), statistics reveal shocking levels of violence against women in the Arab regions. Although Faten Hamama is not responsible for these statistics, it is still tremendously wrong for such a fragile and impotent female type to become a symbol of femininity in any way. Such role models are exactly the ones who receive daily smacks of "legitimate" violence.

Unlike Faten Hamama, Sanaa Gamil was not only a movie star, but also, more importantly, one of the best Egyptian theater actresses. She has also played a number of roles on the French stage for *La Comedie Francaise*.[165] Her performance is regarded by many critics as superior to that of most cinema and theater artists, although she did not became an icon or a first lady of any screen, for her physical features were considered coarse and her roles were not stereotyped as fragile and powerless girls. The roles she played throughout her life did not embody the Eastern type of female weakness, thus public opinion, following the folkloric social norms, was not ready to fit her into its mindset, as this might have led to a sort of revolution that could destabilize the whole society in the long term. Therefore, the admired female type remains the same despite all social changes that hit the Arab communities: an obedient woman who is subject to all kinds of violence, both "legitimate" and non-legitimate.

Dramatically, Arabs have flirted with the shy eyes of woman. They have written thousands of poems praising her blushing cheeks and bashfulness. They even worship women who "have no voice," and those who "have a mouth in order to eat and not to talk," and those who are "obedient, silent and powerless." Arabic proverbs have flattered both "the fast ride" and "the obedient woman," so how then, for God's sake, is a woman like Sanaa Gamil, overloaded with talent and education, to become an example to follow in our sad Arabic world?

❦

Let us admit that our problem, as Arabs, is not with the laws that promote and facilitate violence, but with the concept of "law" in particular, which does not really stem from the ideal view of our human survival, a sacred notion that we are unable to develop, handle, or reconsider. Our laws remain static, without mass, without wavelength, and without a location in space. This is the definition of "zero."

Violence against woman cannot be eliminated without political will at the highest level. The expression of this will and the condemnation of this violence can be done in such ways as legislation, national work plans, allocation of adequate resources, and persistent efforts to overcome impunity, i.e. exemption from punishment. Moreover, a suitable environment is very much needed for non-governmental organizations to do effective work on this issue.

States must fulfill their duty towards human rights, regulate relations between women and men, and mediate any other system associated with them. These states must also cooperate with civil society organizations publically and transparently to oppose this violence and, most importantly, to look into the eyes of this "being" whose name is Woman and who was, once upon a time, hovering over the face of the waters with God's word.

GLOSSARY

[1] The Hijab is a veil that covers the head and chest, which is particularly worn by a Muslim female beyond the age of puberty in the presence of adult males. "Hijab." ~ *Wikipedia.org*

[2] Kahf, Mohja. *From Royal Body the Robe was Removed: The Blessings of the Veil and the Trauma of Forced Unveiling in the Middle East.* (Oakland: University of California Press, 2008), 27.

[3] The Lisān al-'Arab ("The Arab Tongue") was completed by Ibn Manzur in 1290. Occupying 20 printed book volumes (in the most frequently cited edition), it is the most well-known dictionary of the Arabic language. "Ibn Manzur." ~ *Wikipedia.org*

[4] Halal:
Religiously acceptable according to Islamic law. ~ *OxfordDictionaries.com*

[5] Haram:
Forbidden or proscribed by Islamic law. ~ *OxfordDictionaries.com*

[6] Huda (or Hoda) Sha`arawi (1879 –1947), was a pioneering Egyptian feminist leader and nationalist. Sha`arawi founded and became the first president of the Egyptian Feminist Union. "Huda Sha'arawi." ~ *Wikipedia.org*

[7] Blackstone, Sir William. *Commentaries on the Laws of England: in Four Books; with an Analysis of the Works, Vol. 1.* (New York: Harper & Brothers, 1852), 40.

[8] A civic culture or civic political culture is a political culture characterized by "acceptance of the authority of the state" and "a belief in participation in civic duties. "Civic Political Culture" ~ *Wikipedia.com*

[9] Rozental, Mark Moiseevich. *A Dictionary of Philosophy.* Moscow: Progress Publishers, 1967.

[10] *Al Wasat News.* September 11, 2007.

[11] Jacques Marie Émile Lacan (1901 –1981) was a French psychoanalyst and psychiatrist who has been called "the most controversial psycho-analyst since Freud." Giving yearly seminars in Paris from 1953 to 1981, Lacan influenced France's intellectuals in the 1960s and the 1970s, especially the post-structuralist philosophers. His interdisciplinary work was as a "self-proclaimed Freudian" and featured the unconscious, the castration complex, the ego, identification, and language as subjective perception. His ideas have had a significant impact on critical theory, literary theory, 20th-century French philosophy, sociology, feminist theory, film theory, and clinical psychoanalysis. "Jacques Lacan." ~ *Wikipedia.org*

[12] Alyan, Dr. Saiid Suleiman. *Women in the Old Testament: A Study of Pedigrees and Meanings.* (Cairo: Madbouly Library,1996), 4.

[13] Lichen:
An organism that is formed by the symbiotic association of a fungus and an alga or cyanobacterium and occurs as crusty patches or bushy growths on tree trunks, bare ground, etc. ~ *Dictionary.com*.

[14] Ijtihad:
An Islamic legal term that means "independent reasoning" or "the utmost effort an individual can put forth in an activity. "Ijtihad." ~ *Wikipedia.org*

[15] Scheherazade was a legendary Persian queen and the storyteller of *One Thousand and One Nights.* The story goes that every day Shahryar (Persian for "king") would marry a new virgin, and after doing so would dispatch the previous day's wife to be beheaded. This was done in anger, having found out that his first wife was unfaithful to him. He had killed 1,000 such women by the time he was introduced to Scheherazade, the vizier's daughter. "Scheherazade." ~ *Wikipedia.org*

[16] Haremlik Turkey:
Means the private portion of the house, the family rooms, as opposed to the saremlik, the public area or reception rooms. "Haremlik." ~ *Wikipedia.org*

[17] I'm paraphrasing from the Bible: "In the beginning, God created the heavens and the earth. The earth was without form, and void; and darkness was on the face of the deep. And the Spirit of God was hovering over the face of the waters." (Gen. 1:1-2)

[18] Khadīja bint Khuwaylid or Khadija the great (circa 555–620 CE) was the first wife of the Islamic prophet Muhammad. She is commonly regarded by Muslims as the "mother of Islam" and was the first person to convert to Islam. "Khadija." ~ *Wikipedia.org*

[19] Fatimah Zahra (c. 605 or 615– 633) was a daughter of the Islamic prophet Muhammad and Khadijah, wife of Ali and mother of Hasan and Hussein, and one of the five members of Ahl al-Bayt. She became the object of great veneration by all Muslims because she lived closest to her father and supported him in his difficulties, because of the historical importance of her husband and her two sons, and because she is the only member of Prophet Muhammad's family that gave him descendants, numerously spread through the Islamic world. For Muslims, Fatimah is an inspiring example and Fatimah is one of the most popular girl's names throughout the Muslim world. (Rogerson, Barnaby. *The Heirs Of The Prophet Muhammad: And The Roots Of The Sunni-Shia Schism*. London: Abacus, 2006.)

[20] Rābiʿa al-ʿAdawiyya al-Qaysiyya (717–801 C.E.) was a female Muslim saint and Sufi mystic. "Rabiʾa al-Adawiyya." ~ *Wikipedia.org*

[21] Asmāʾ bint Abu Bakr (c. 592-692 CE) was one of the companions of the Islamic prophet Muhammad. Bewley, A. *The Women of Madina: Muhammad ibn Saad, Tabaqat, Vol. 8.* (London: Ta-Ha Publishers, 1995), 193.

[22] Khawlah bint al-Azwar was a prominent woman from Prophet Muhammad's lifetime. She was a Muslim Arab warrior, sister of Zirrar ibn Azwar, the legendary Muslim soldier and commander of the Rashidun army during the 7th century Muslim conquest. "Khawlah bint al-Azwar." ~ *Wikipedia.org*

[23] Faten Hamama (1931-2015) was an Egyptian film and television actress and producer. She made her screen debut in 1939, when she was only seven years old. "Faten Hamama." ~ *Wikipedia.org*

[24] Marie-Jeanne Phlippon Roland (1754–1793), better known simply as Madame Roland and born Marie-Jeanne Phlippon, was, together with her husband Jean-Marie Roland de la Platière, a supporter of the French Revolution and influential member of the Girondist faction. She fell out of

favor during the Reign of Terror and died on the guillotine. "Madame Roland." ~ *Wikipedia.org*

[25] Anne Louise Germaine de Staël-Holstein (1766–1817), commonly known as Madame de Staël, was a French woman of letters of Swiss origin whose lifetime overlapped with the events of the French Revolution and the Napoleonic era. "Germaine de Staël." ~ *Wikipedia.org*

[26] Helen Adams Keller (1880–1968) was an American author, political activist, and lecturer. She was the first deaf/blind person to earn a bachelor of arts degree. "Helen Keller." ~ *Wikipedia.org*

[27] Sanaa Gamil (1930-2002), born Thoraya Youssef Atallah, was an Egyptian actress. Born to a Coptic Orthodox family in Upper Egypt, she moved to Cairo to pursue her acting career and changed her name to Sanaa Gamil. "Sanaa Gamil." ~ *Wikipedia.org*

[28] Romanyshyn, Robert. *Mirror and Metaphor: Images and Stories of Psychological Life.* Lake Charles: Trivium Publishing, 2001.

[29] Adonis. *The Book, The Rhetoric and The Hijab.* (Lebanon: Dar al-Adab Publishing House, 2009) p.18.

[30] Ibn Taymiyyah (1263-1328), one of Islam's most forceful theologians who, as a member of the Pietist school founded by Ibn Hanbal, sought the return of the Islamic religion to its sources: the Qur'ān and the sunnah. "Ibn Taymiyyah." *Encyclopaedia Britannica.*
http://www.britannica.com/biography/Ibn-Taymiyyah

[31] Daco, Pierre. *Comprehend Women and Their Profound Psychology.* (Bulgaria: Colibri Books, 2006), 313.

[32] Ibid.

[33] Dr. Emmons' research is at the interface of personality psychology, the psychology of emotion and the psychology of religion. His primary interests are in the psychology of gratitude and the psychology of personal goals, and how each is related to positive psychological processes, including happiness,

well-being, and personality integration. "Robert Emmons." UC Davis Psychology. *http://psychology.ucaavis.edu/faculty/emmons/*

[34] Mr. Al-Jaber is considered one of the major intellectual figures in the contemporary Arab world and is known for his academic project "The Critique of the Arab Mind." He published several influential books on the Arab philosophical tradition. Al-Jaber, Mohammed Abed. *The Structure of the Arab Mind.* (Beirut: Centre for Arab Unity Studies, 1986), 45. "Mohammed Abed al-Jabri" - *Wikipedia.org*

[35] Ibid., 46.

[36] *Concise Dictionary of Philosophy.* (Moscow: Progress Publishers, 1954), 511.

[37] The superego is the ethical component of the personality and provides the moral standards by which the ego operates. The superego's criticisms, prohibitions, and inhibitions form a person's conscience, and its positive aspirations and ideals represent one's idealized self-image, or "ego ideal." "Super ego." *Encyclopaedia Britannica.* *http://www.britannica.com/EBchecked/topic/574274/superego*

[38] Al-Bukhārī is one of the Kutub al-Sittah (six major hadith collections) of Sunni Islam. These prophetic traditions, or hadith, were collected by the Persian Muslim scholar Muhammad Al-Bukhari, after being transmitted orally for generations. Sunni Muslims view this as one of the three most trusted collections of hadith along with Sahih Muslim and Muwatta Imam Malik. In some circles, it is considered the most authentic book after the Quran. The Arabic word "sahih" translates as "authentic or correct." Brown, Jonathan. *The Canonization of Al-Bukhari and Muslim: The Formation and Function of the Sunni Hadith Canon.* The Netherlands: Brill, 2007.

[39] Sahih Muslim (full title Al-Musnadu Al-Sahihu bi Naklil Adli) is one of the Kutub al-Sittah (six major ahadith) of the hadith in Sunni Islam. It is the second most authentic hadith collection after Sahih al-Bukhari, and is highly acclaimed by Sunni Muslims. It was collected by Muslim ibn al-Hajjaj, also known as Imam Muslim. "Sahih." *Islamic Dictionary.* *http://www.islamic-dictionary.com/index.php?word=sahih*

[40] Jami' al-Tirmidhi is a collection of hadith compiled by Imam Abu Eisa al-Tirmidhi. His collection is unanimously considered to be one of the six famous collections of hadith (al-Kutub al-Sittah), and contains roughly 4400 hadiths (with repetitions) in 46 chapters. Adam al-Kawthari, Mufti Muhammad ibn. "Imam Tirmidhi and his Al-Jami' al-Sunan." *Daruliftaa.* *http://daruliftaa.com/node/7130*

[41] Sunan an-Nasa'i is a collection of hadith compiled by Imam Ahmad an-Nasa'i (rahimahullah). His collection is unanimously considered to be one of the six canonical collections of hadith (Kutub as-Sittah) of the Sunnah of the Prophet. It contains roughly 5700 hadith (with repetitions) in 52 books. "Sunan an-Nasa'i." Sunnah. *http://sunnah.com/nasai*

[42] Sunan Ibn Majah is one of the Kutub al-Sittah (six major hadiths), collected by Ibn Mājah. "Sunan Ibn Mājah." ‑ *Wikipedia.org*

[43] Halāl is an Arabic word for any object or an action which is permissible to use or engage in, according to Islamic law. The term covers and designates not only food and drink but also all matters of daily life. The opposite of this word is haram. Quran 7:157

[44] Harām is an Arabic term meaning sinful. In Islamic Jurisprudence, haram is used to refer to any act that is forbidden by Allah, and is one of five categories that define the morality of human action. Adamec, Ludwig. *Historical Dictionary of Islam, 2nd ed.* (Lanham: Scarecrow Press, 2009), 102.

[45] Al-da'if: It is a hadith that does not have the qualities of either al-hasan or al-sahih.

[46] Al-hasan: It is a report whose collector and transmitters are well known. It is the most regular hadith, and most scholars accept it.

[47] Al-sahih: It is a hadith free of any faults, related by several continuous chains of veracious transmitters with more than one first recorder.

[48] Al-marfu': It is a hadith which reaches one of the Ma'sumun, regardless of continuity in the chain of transmitters.

[49] Al-mawdu': It is a tradition forged by its narrator.

[50] Al-mutawatir: It is a tradition which has been transmitted from several narrators, so that it is impossible that it should have been forged. There are two kinds of this hadith: mutawatir in meaning, and mutawatir in words. However, if recurrence (tawatur) is in words, there may be chances of forgery.

[51] The sanad and matn are the primary elements of a hadith (a collection of traditions and sayings from the prophet Muhammad, which is the main source of Muslim guidance). The sanad is the information provided regarding the route by which the matn has been reached. It is so named due to the reliance of the hadith specialists upon it in determining the authenticity or weakness of a hadith. The term sanad is synonymous with the similar term isnad (a companion of the prophet). The matn is the actual wording of the hadith by which its meaning is established, or stated differently, the objective at which the sanad arrives at, consisting of speech. Al-Suyuti, Jalaluddin. *Tadrib al-Rawi, Vol. 1.* (Lebanon: Dar al-Kitab al-Arabi, 2006), 39-41.

[52] The Hadith is where Muslims determine the Sunnah (or way) of the prophet, which is Muhammad's words, actions, and practices. This is key to Islam since Muslims are commanded to obey and emulate him, so even the most insignificant of actions on his part have a drastic effect upon the doctrines and laws of Islam. "Hadith." ~ *Wikipedia.org*

[53] Logos: The Greek word logos (traditionally meaning word, thought, principle, or speech) has been used among both philosophers and theologians. In most of its usages, logos is marked by two main distinctions - the first dealing with human reason (the rationality in the human mind which seeks to attain universal understanding and harmony), the second with universal intelligence (the universal ruling force governing and revealing through the cosmos to humankind, i.e., the Divine). "Logos." *PBS. http://www.pbs.org/faithandreason/theogloss/logos-body.html*

[54] Ibid.

[55] Stoicism: an ancient Greek school of philosophy founded at Athens by Zeno of Citium. The school taught that virtue, the highest good, is based on knowledge, and that the wise live in harmony with the divine Reason (also identified with Fate and Providence) that governs nature, and are indifferent

to the vicissitudes of fortune and to pleasure and pain. "Stoicism." - *Oxford Dictionaries.*

[56] Tripolitis, Antonia. *Religions of the Hellenistic-Roman Age.* (Grand Rapids: Wm. B. Eerdmans Publishing Co., 2001), 37-38.

[57] Anima Mundi: The world soul is, according to several systems of thought, an intrinsic connection between all living things on the planet, which relates to our world in much the same way as the soul is connected to the human body. "Anima Mundi" - *Wikipedia*

[58] Lindsay, James. *Studies in European Philosophy.* (City: Hesperides Press, 2006), 53.

[59] *Cambridge Dictionary of Philosophy, 2nd ed.,* "Philo Judaeus."

[60] Copleston, Frederick. *A History of Philosophy, Vol. 1.* (London: Continuum, 2003), 458–462.

[61] Philo, *De Profugis,* cited in Gerald Friedlander, *Hellenism and Christianity,* P. Vallentine, 1912, pp. 114–115.

[62] Stace, W. T. (1960) The Teachings of the Mystics, New York, Signet, pp110-123

[63] Ibn Khaldūn (1332 AD – 1406 AD) was an Arab Muslim historiographer and historian, regarded to be among the founding fathers of modern historiography, sociology and economics. "Ibn Khaldun." - *Wikipedia.org*

[64] Khaldun, Ibn. *The Muqaddimah.* Revive of the Arab Heritage Publishing House, p. 496.

[65] "To reassure my heart' of Mohamed Al talibi (Part I, the faith) P, 16. Dar Saras publishing , Tunisia 2007

[66] Ibid., 17.

[67] Abd Ar Rahman bin Muhammed ibn Khaldun. *The Muqaddimah.* Translated by Franz Rosenthal. (Princeton: Princeton Univ Press, 1988), 545.

[68] John 6:60, 7:36, 8:37,43, 12:48, 19:8

[69] Clark, Gordon H. "God and Logic." *The Trinity Foundation.* *http://www.trinityfoundation.org/journal.php?id=16*

[70] Harris, Stephen L. *Understanding the Bible.* (Palo Alto: Mayfield. 1985), 302-310.

[71] Ratzinger, Joseph. "Europe in the Crisis of Cultures." *The Way.* *www.theway.org.uk/endeanweb/ratzinger32-2.pdf*

[72] Gaetani, Roger and Jean-Louise Michon. *Sufism: Love and Wisdom.* Indiana: World Wisdom, 2006.

[73] Ibn Arabī (1165–1240) was an Arab Andalusian Sufi mystic and philosopher. He is renowned by some practitioners of Sufism as "the greatest master" and also as a genuine saint. "Ibn Arabi." ~ *Wikipedia.org*

[74] Frazee, Charles A. "Ibn al-'Arabī and Spanish Mysticism of the Sixteenth Century". In *Numen* Vol. 14 (3), 229–240. The Netherlands, Brill, 1967.

[75] Ibn al-'Arabi uses no less than twenty-two different terms to describe the various aspects under which this single Logos may be viewed. Little, J.T. "Al-Insān al-Kāmil: The perfect man according to Ibn al-'Arabī." In *The Muslim World,* Vol. 77, 43–54. Wiley Online Library. 1987.

[76] Taphophobia
    Fear of being buried alive. ~ *Dictionary.com*

[77] Milner, Dr. Larry Stephan. *Hardness of Heart Hardness of Life: The Stain of Human Infanticide.* (Lanham, MD: University Press America, 2000), 122.

[78] Hiding from the people because of the evil of the tidings; "Will he keep her with disgrace, or bury her beneath the earth?"; pay heed! Very evil is the judgment they impose! (Nahl 16:59)

Indeed ruined are those who slay their children out of senseless ignorance and forbid the sustenance which Allah has bestowed upon them, in order to fabricate lies against Allah; they have undoubtedly gone astray and not attained the path. (Ana`am 6:140)

Abd Allaah (bin Masud) said, "I asked Apostle of Allaah which sin is the gravest?" He replied, "That you associate someone with Allaah, while He has created you." I again asked, "Which then?" He replied, "That you commit adultery with the wife of your neighbor." Allaah then revealed the following Qur'anic verse in support of the statement of the Prophet: "Those who invoke not with Allaah any other god nor slay such life as Allaah has made sacred except for just cause nor commit fornication." -Sunan Abi Dawud » Divorce (Kitab Al-Talaq).
http://www.searchtruth.com/book_display.php?book=12&translator=3

[79] Exod., 20:17

[80] Exod., 21:7

[81] Judg., 11:29-40

[82] Ps., 51:7

[83] John, 8:7

[84] "Jesus Forgives a Woman Taken in Adultery." Bible Gateway.
http://www.biblegateway.com/resources/commentaries/IVP-NT/John/Jesus-Forgives-Woman-Taken

[85] Ibid.

[86] "Morning Service." *Sacred Texts.*
http://www.sacrea-texts.com/jud/spb/spb05.htm

[87] An expression that means "all the Arab countries."

[88] "It has been narrated through a different chain of transmitters, on the authority of Hudhaifa b. al-Yaman who said:

Messenger of Allah, no doubt, we had an evil time (i.e. the days of Jahiliyya or ignorance) and God brought us a good time (i. e. Islamic period) through which we are now living. Will there be a bad time after this good time? He (the Holy Prophet) said: Yes. I said: Will there be a good time after this bad time? He said: Yes. I said: Will there be a bad time after good time? He said: Yes. I said: How? Whereupon he said: There will be leaders who will not be led by my guidance and who will not adopt my ways. There will be among them men who will have the hearts of devils in the bodies of human beings. I said: What should I do. Messenger of Allah, if I (happen) to live in that time? He replied: You will listen to the Amir and carry out his orders; even if your back is flogged and your wealth is snatched, you should listen and obey." "Hadith Collection: Sahih Muslim/Book-33/Hadith-81." *The Quran.* *http://quranx.com/Hadith/muslim/Book-33/Hadith-81/*

[89] "Narrated `Ikrima: Some Zanadiqa (atheists) were brought to `Ali and he burnt them. The news of this event, reached Ibn `Abbas who said, "If I had been in his place, I would not have burnt them, as Allah's Messenger forbade it, saying, 'Do not punish anybody with Allah's punishment (fire).' I would have killed them according to the statement of Allah's Messenger, 'Whoever changed his Islamic religion, then kill him.'" "Hadith Collection: Sahih Bukhari/Book-88/Hadith-5." *The Quran.* *http://quranx.com/Hadith/bukhari/Book-88/Hadith-5/*

[90] Umar, also spelled Omar, was one of the most powerful and influential Muslim caliphs in history. He was a senior Sahaba of the Islamic prophet Muhammad. He succeeded Abu Bakr as the second caliph of the Rashidun Caliphate on 23 August 634. "Umar Ibn Al Khattab" - *Wikipedia.*

[91] Mernissi, Fatima. *Dreams of Trespass: Tales of a Harem Girlhood.* (Casablanca: Fenak Publishing House), 73.

[92] Ibid., 110

[93] *Delaying The Sunset* was originally written in 2008 and published in 2009 in Damascus, Syria. Since the war against Syria, things have changed dramatically, as 89 nations around the globe sent their mercenaries to destroy the country under the pretext of introducing freedom and democracy.

[94] Abu Hamid al-Ghazali: As the author of some 250 books on topics ranging from theology and ethics to metaphysics and philosophy, al-Ghazali came to be known as 'Proof of Islam.' "Al-Ghazali: The Alchemy of Happiness." *Galactic Resonance.*
http://www.galacticresonance.org/al-ghazali-the-alchemist-of-happiness/

[95] Ayatullah Jafar Subhani. The Concepts of Islam, Vol. 5. Ahlulbayt Organization. P 346.

[96] (Baqarah 2:124) And (remember) when Ibrahim's (Abraham's) Lord tested him in some matters and he fulfilled them; He said, "I am going to appoint you as a leader for mankind"; invoked Ibrahim, "And of my offspring"; He said, "My covenant does not include the unjust (wrong-doers)."

[97] Gautama Buddha, also known as Siddhārtha Gautama,[Shakyamuni, or simply the Buddha], was a sage on whose teachings Buddhism was founded. "Guatama Buddha." - *Wikipedia.org*

[98] Harissa is a mountain village in Lebanon. "Harissa, Lebanon." - *Wikipedia.org*

[99] Ziad Rahbani (born 1956 -) is a Lebanese composer and a writer (for radio shows and theatre). "Ziad Rahbani." *Wafa Music.*
http://www.wafamusic.com/Liban/ziad-rahbani/ziad-rahbani-308.htm

[100] This book was written in 2009 before the so-called Arab spring started and things began to change in Syria, where freedom is now available to all people per the national constitution.

[101] "East Asian History Sourcebook." *Fordham University: The Jesuit University of New York.*
http://www.fordham.edu/halsall/eastasia/eastasiasbook.asp

[102] Swami Vivekananda (1863-1902) born Narendranath Dutta, was an Indian Hindu monk and chief disciple of the 19th-century Indian mystic Ramakrishna Paramahansa. "Swami Vivekananda" – *Wikipedia*

[103] "Vivekananda: Sexual Force." *Sacred Sex.*
http://sacrea-sex.org/scriptures/hinduism/37-vivekananda-sexual-force.html

[104] "The Canons of the Holy Fathers Assembled at Gangra." *Orthodox Church Fathers.*
http://orthodoxchurchfathers.com/fathers/npnf214/npnf2139.htm#P2082_4189 37

[105] John Eastburn Boswell (1947 – 1994) was a prominent historian and a professor at Yale University. Many of Boswell's studies focused on the issue of religion and homosexuality, specifically Christianity and homosexuality. "John Boswell." - *Wikipedia.org*

[106] The King James Bible (KJV)

[107] John, Chapter 8

[108] Cor., 6:19

[109] Cor., 7:9

[110] St. Augustin: Anti-Pelagian Writings, tr. Peter Holmes, Robert Ernest Wallace and Benjamin B. Warfield. Select Library of Nicene and Post-Nicene Fathers, Ser. 1, Vol. V (New York, 1893). Book I, Chapter 5.

[111] Saint Augustine of Hippo. *Basic Writings of St. Augustine*. Edited by Whitney J. Oates. (Ada, MI: Baker Publishing Group, 1993), 455.

[112] Saint Augustine of Hippo. *The City of God*. Translated by Henry Bettenson. (Harmondsworth, England: Penguin Books, 1972), 21.

[113] Russell, Bertrand. *Marriage and Morals*, (Amherst, NY: Prometheus Books, 1970), 64.

[114] Lecky, William Edward Hartpole. *History of European Morals,* Vol. 2. (Bel Air, CA: University Press of the Pacific, 2012), 350-351.

[115] al-Hur al-Aamili, Shaikh. *Wasā'il al-Shī a*, part 20, P. 108.

[116] Al-sīra is the Arabic term used for the various traditional Muslim biographies of Muhammad from which, in addition to the Quran and Hadith, most historical information about his life and the early period of Islam is derived. "Prophetic Biography." ~ *Wikipedia.org*

[117] *One Thousand and One Nights* is a collection of West and South Asian stories and folk tales compiled in Arabic during the Islamic Golden Age. It is often known in English as the Arabian Nights. "One Thousand and One Nights." ~ *Wikipedia.org*

[118] *The Perfumed Garden of Sensual Delight* by Muhammad ibn Muhammad al-Nafzawi is a fifteenth-century Arabic sex manual and work of erotic literature. The book presents opinions on what qualities men and women should have to be attractive, gives advice on sexual technique, warnings about sexual health, and recipes to remedy sexual maladies. "The Perfumed Garden." ~ *Wikipedia.org*

[119] Tarabishi, George. *Critique of the critique of Arab Mind.* Beirut: Al Saki Publishing House, 2011.

[120] Ibid., 73.

[121] Ibid., 75.

[122] al-Jāhiz, in full Abū 'Uthmān 'Amr ibn Bahr al-Jāhiz (c. 776—868/869), Islamic theologian, intellectual, and litterateur known for his individual and masterful Arabic prose. "al-Jāhiz." *Encyclopaedia Britannica.* *http://www.britannica.com/EBchecked/topic/299421/al-Jahiz*

[123] al-Jāḥiẓ. *Kitab al-Bayan wa al-Tabyin (The Book of eloquence and Oratory), Vol. 3.* p. 20.

[124] Jahiliyyah is an Islamic concept of "ignorance of divine guidance" or "the state of ignorance of the guidance from God" or "Days of Ignorance", referring to the condition in which Arabs found themselves in pre-Islamic Arabia. *A Concise Dictionary of Koranic Arabic.* Wiesbaden, Germany: Reichert Verlag, 2004.

[125] Sā'id al-Andalusī (1029–1070) was a historian, philosopher of science and thought, and mathematical scientist with a special interest in astronomy. "Said Al-Andalusi." ~ *Wikipedia.org*

[126] *Science in the Medieval World: Book of the Categories of Nations* by Sa'id al-Andalusi is a medieval Spanish Muslim manuscript describing the contributions of nine nations to human knowledge. "Science in the Medieval World." *University of Texas Press.* *http://utpress.utexas.edu/index.php/books/alasci#sthash.73beXKDj.dpuf*

[127] "Sharia" is the code of law derived from the Quran and from the teachings and example of Mohammed; "sharia is only applicable to Muslims"; "under Islamic law there is no separation of church and state." "Sharia." *The Free Dictionary. http://www.thefreedictionary.com/sharia*

[128] Al-Mansur or Abu Ja'far Abdallah ibn Muhammad al-Mansur (95 AH–158 AH/714 AD–775 AD) was the second Abbasid Caliph from 136 AH to 158 AH (754 AD – 775 AD) .He is generally regarded as the real founder of the Abbasid Caliphate. "Al-Mansur." ~ *Wikipedia.org*

[129] al-Andalusi, Sa'id. *Science in the Medieval World: Book of the Categories of Nations.* (Austin, TX: University of Texas Press, 1996), 128 -129.

[130] Today, with all that is going on in the Middle East (what has been called an "Arab spring"), people have started to question the feasibility of any religion, not only Islam, in keeping social order in good shape and protecting its workability.

[131] Ibn Rushd Abu'l Walid Muhammad (1126-98) (Averroes) is regarded by many as the most important of the Islamic philosophers. A product of twelfth-century Islamic Spain, he set out to integrate Aristotelian philosophy with Islamic thought. "Ibn Rushd Abu'l Walid Muhammad." *Islamic Philosophy Online.* *http://www.muslimphilosophy.com/ir/art/ibn%20rushd-rep.html*

[132] "Harem virus" means "harem effect or syndrome" and is a made-up phrase by Moroccan author and feminist Fatima Mernissi in her book *Dreams of Trespass: Tales of a Harem Girlhood.* New York: Perseus Books, 1995.

[133] Nietzsche, Friedrich. *Beyond Good and Evil*. London, Penguin Publishing Group, 1973, section 232.

[134] "Thomas Aquinas on the Generation of Women." *Women Can Be Priests*. *http://www.womenpriests.org/theology/aqui_wom.asp*

[135] "On the Generation of Animals." (Book IV, Section 6.) *http://ebooks.adelaide.edu.au/a/aristotle/generation/book4.html*

[136] Plato, the republic, Book V, published by Allan Bloom, USA, 1991

[137] Tawfiq al-Hakim or Tawfik el-Hakim (1898–1987) was a prominent Egyptian writer. He is one of the pioneers of the Arabic novel and drama. "Tawfiq al-Hakim." ~ *Wikipedia.org*

[138] Lawful and unlawful.

[139] "Adolf Hitler: Biography and Character." *Broadcast PDF Documents*. *http://pdfcast.org/pdf/adolj-hitler-biography-and-character*

[140] Ibid.

[141] Secretary-General of the United Nations. "Ending Violence Against Women: From Words to Action, Study of the Secretary-General." (Herndon, VA: United Nations Publication, 2006), 53.

[142] Marxist terminology, meaning the raw materials and means of labor used in the production process.

[143] Secretary-General of the United Nations. "Ending Violence Against Women: From Words to Action, Study of the Secretary-General." (Herndon, VA: United Nations Publication, 2006), 15.

[144] Ibid., 23.

[145] Ibid.

[146] See: Harway, M. and James O'Neil, eds. *What Causes Men's Violence Against Women?* Thousand Oaks: Sage Publications, 1999; WHO. *Multi-*

Country Stuay on Women's Health and Domestic Violence Against Women: Initial Results on Prevalence, Health Outcomes and Women's Responses. Geneva: World Health Organization, 2005; and WHO. *World Report On Violence and Health.* Geneva, World Health Organization, 2002.

[147] Secretary-General of the United Nations. "Ending Violence Against Women: From Words to Action, Study of the Secretary-General." (Herndon, VA: United Nations Publication, 2006), 46.

[148] Ibid., 28.

[149] Raday, Frances. "Culture, religion and gender." Oxford University Press and New York University School of Law 2003, I.CON, Volume 1, Number 4, 2003, pp 663-715.

[150] Ibid.

[151] Merry, S. E.. "Constructing a Global Law—Violence Against Women and the Human Rights System." Law & Social Inquiry Volume 28, Issue 4, pages 941–977, October 2003.

[152] Secretary-General of the United Nations. "Ending Violence Against Women: From Words to Action, Study of the Secretary-General." (Herndon, VA: United Nations Publication, 2006), 32.

[153] During the war in Syria, which has lasted for almost 3 years now (2011-present), violence against woman in the country has risen dramatically as part of the hysterical scene of war. This has not always been the case in Syria, and therefore the recent statistics are to be regarded as an inadequate evaluation about violence against women in Syria.

[154] The study covered 1,891 families. General Union of Women, Syrian Commission for Family Affairs, Violence against women study: Syria, supported by the United Nations Development Fund for Women, 2005. Secretary-General of the United Nations. "Ending Violence Against Women: From Words to Action, Study of the Secretary-General." (Herndon, VA: United Nations Publication, 2006), 38.

[155] Saltzman, L., Fanslow, J. L., and others. "Intimate partner violence surveillance: Uniform definitions and recommended data elements, version 1.0." Atlanta: Centers for Disease Control and Prevention, National Center for Injury Prevention and Control, 2002.

[156] Secretary-General of the United Nations. "Ending Violence Against Women: From Words to Action, Study of the Secretary-General." (Herndon, VA: United Nations Publication, 2006), 39.

[157] Ibid.

[158] UNFPA, State of World Population 2000 (New York, UNFPA, 2000); Kogacioglu, D., 2004. "The tradition effect: Framing honor crimes in Turkey", Differences: A Journal of Feminist Cultural Studies, vol. 15, No. 2 (2004), pp. 119-151.

[159] Secretary-General of the United Nations. "Ending Violence Against Women: From Words to Action, Study of the Secretary-General." (Herndon, VA: United Nations Publication, 2006), 43.

[160] Ibid., 44.

[161] See E/CN.4/1998/54; E/CN.4/2004/66/Add.1; Human Rights Watch, All too familiar: Sexual abuse of women in U.S. state prisons (1996); Arbour, L. Commission of Inquiry into certain events at the Prison for women in Kingston (Public Works and Government Services, Canada, 1996).

[162] Although such exaggeration certainly exists in daily human life. – Author's note.

[164] Culler, Jonathan. *Literary Theory: A Very Short Introduction.* (Chicago: Stanford University Press, 2007), 137.

[165] The Comédie-Française is one of the few state theatres in France. It is the only state theatre to have its own troupe of actors. "Comédie Française." – *Wikipedia.org*

About the Author

Gladys Matar grew up in an environment ideally suited for nurturing the growth of her artistic and literary talents from an early age. In Latakia, the city with the distinction of being the most important port of Syria, Ms. Matar attended Les Carmelites catholic school from kindergarten through middle school, and then moved to the public school system following legislative changes that prohibited private religious schools. Later, she attended the foreign literature program at the University of Latakia, graduating in 1984 with a degree in French Literature.

Ms. Matar has published ten books to date, with several more currently under production for future publication. She is a playwright and screenwriter, and regularly publishes articles on literary critique and world politics in a multitude of Arabic periodicals and reputable literary websites.

She has been awarded and celebrated by many nationally and internationally distinguished cultural associations and organizations.

Her time is dedicated to research, writing, translating and delivering lectures on current world affairs. She also produces works for others and is perhaps one of the few ghostwriters in the Arab World.

To see Ms. Matar's other books please visit her website.

www.gladysmatar.net

www.ingramcontent.com/pod-product-compliance
Lightning Source LLC
Chambersburg PA
CBHW031155270326
41931CB00006B/280